CREATING MANDALAS

WITH SACRED

GEOMETRY

CREATING MANDALAS
WITH
SACRED GEOMETRY

COLOR AND DRAW MANDALAS

USING ANCIENT PRINCIPLES

Susanne F. Fincher

Shambhala
Boulder
2017

Shambhala Publications, Inc.
2129 13th Street
Boulder, Colorado 80302
www.shambhala.com

9 8 7 6 5 4 3

Printed in the United States of America

Shambhala Publications makes every effort to print on
acid-free, recycled paper.

Shambhala Publications is distributed worldwide by
Penguin Random House, Inc., and its subsidiaries.

Designed by Gopa & Ted2, Inc.

ISBN: 978-1-61180-326-6

CONTENTS

INTRODUCTION

MY EARLIEST MEMORY of creating a mandala with geometry is a spring project I completed for my junior high geometry class. I remember that the instructions were to use the skills we had learned in class to construct a geometric design inside a circle on a 12-inch x 12-inch piece of plywood. Then, our teacher explained, we would hammer small nails into the wood, delineating our design. Finally, we would tightly wrap colored thread from nail to nail to complete our work. Needless to say, our parents helped, but the pleasure of creating and sharing the projects enlivened our class for weeks. (See youtube.com for the tutorial, "How to Create a Colorful Spirograph String Art.")

Mandalas are circular designs that suggest spiritual and psychological meanings. At the level of individual psychology, the circular form of a mandala conveys a feeling of safety associated with early experiences of nurturing. The mandala reflects a person's felt experience of being a *self*: a locus of awareness, a generator of willed activity, a creature with memories of its own unique history. In short, a mandala mirrors personal identity, persistent yet always in flux. Individuals find pleasure in creating and coloring their own mandalas for creative self-expression, psychological insight, and an experience of balance, harmony, and well-being.

The circle that is the basis of mandalas has rich artistic and cultural resonance. At the most basic level, a circle offers a structured graphic space to enter, in contrast to the stark challenge of a blank, unmarked piece of paper. Visually, a circle can bring order to what would otherwise be random scribbles. Viewed as a line without end, a circle suggests the enduring continuity of time itself. For aboriginal peoples, drawing a circle on the ground demarks a sacred space of sanctuary. Circles are the basis of fabulous structures, both ancient and modern, built for religious, scientific, and community purposes. A circle also suggests stability, anchored as it is by a center (seen or unseen), and the synergy of the circle and its center establishes the starting point of sacred geometry.

The term "sacred geometry" (from the Greek *geo* for earth, and *metron* for measurement) refers to certain mathematical techniques used for drawing and the designs made from using those techniques. The designs are imbued with symbolic meanings that are derived from both the meaning of numbers and the historical significance of the finished art. Sacred geometry also refers to drawing as a way of cultivating states of consciousness that contribute to spiritual and psychological self-realization.

This book offers a foundation for understanding sacred geometry, from its beginnings to the significance of numbers and the meaning of symbols in the history of thought. It also provides guidance on how to draw mandalas using geometry.

Creating mandalas in the tradition of sacred geometry can be a pathway toward grasping who you are, where you belong, and what you are to do. This book gives you some useful skills for the journey. Enjoy!

A HISTORY OF NUMBERS

FROM THE EARLIEST TIMES, numbers have been viewed with awe. The ability to count began as an arcane science known to few and was considered powerful, mysterious, and god-like. Numbers, like magic spells, could open the way to desirable outcomes. For example, the Egyptian Book of the Dead revealed that the ferryman who carried the spirit of a dead person across the river to their final home expected his passengers to know how many fingers they had and to prove it by reciting a counting rhyme.

Along with the mystery of numbers, the usefulness of counting has always been highly valued. Around 8000 B.C.E. human beings throughout the ancient world began counting things. They developed special counting sticks, stones, knotted ropes, string, clay bits, and metal pieces to aid them in keeping track of quantities. Numbers, as we know them, had come into being.

Numbers facilitated trade. For example, a handful of marked clay pieces in the hands of a trustworthy dealer could represent goats being offered for sale at market without the goats being physically present. The clay pieces could serve as a record of ownership transfer and justify the new owner's claim to the goats when he resold them to another buyer.

Some of these ancient counting methods survive even today. The use of fingers and other parts of the body for reckoning amounts lives on in the measure we call a *yard,* which was originally the distance from the

Numbers were probably first tallied on fingers. In fact, the word *digit,* meaning "number," is also a word for finger.

tradesman's nose to the tips of the fingers on his right hand. And in the United Kingdom body weight is still measured in terms of *stones* (1 stone is equal to 14 pounds). A woman weighing 140 pounds is said to weigh 10 stone.

Numbers were very useful in ancient Egypt where the annual flooding of the Nile River obliterated property lines. In order to reestablish boundaries, the Egyptians developed ways for measuring plots of land. The work of Egyptian surveyors, known as "rope stretchers" because of the knotted ropes they used, was the beginning of geometry. Many of the tools we use today, such as the divider, compass, and straightedge, were used by the Egyptians in the building of their monumental sacred architecture.

By around 2400 B.C.E., the Egyptians had also developed a 360-day calendar that became the basis for the zodiac. Possibly inspired by the way the sun rises each day at a different point on the horizon line, the 360 days were arranged in a circle that represented one calendar year. Days were grouped into twelve months named after the star constellations visible during that time in the night sky. The circular calendar of 360 days of the year evolved into the idea that *any* circle can be divided into 360 equal portions, or *degrees:* a basic tenet of geometry.

Middle Eastern cultures adopted Egyptian knowledge of geometry and applied it in their sophisticated astronomical observations of the seven visible planets, which they revered as gods. The calculations of their priest-astronomers had practical as well as sacred uses. They determined auspicious dates for ceremonies, advised the best times for planting and harvesting, and warned citizens when to prepare for the flood seasons of their rivers, the Tigris and Euphrates.

Building on the knowledge of their neighbors in Egypt and the Middle East, the Greeks deeply pondered the meaning and significance of numbers. They mastered the operations of division and multiplication as well as addition and subtraction. Despite the limitation of working out calculations by using stones (*calculus* is Greek for "stone") on a smooth surface covered with sand, one Greek sage was able to develop a sophisticated philosophy of numbers. For him, numbers were qualities as well as quantities. He conceptualized numbers as geometric forms imbued with sacred energy, and he considered them the basic building blocks of the cosmos. His name was Pythagoras.

NUMBER IS ALL

Pythagoras was born on the Greek island of Samos in the sixth century B.C.E. Intellectually gifted, he had the good fortune to study with some of the great thinkers of his era in Egypt and Babylon before finally settling in southern Italy, where he attracted followers who embraced his philosophy. Pythagoras is known for the Pythagorean theorem, although he was probably not the first to discover it. During his lifetime, Pythagoras was more famous for his grasp of harmony and proportion that led to the formulation of the golden ratio, also known as the golden mean, golden section, or phi, which became the definition of beauty for centuries to follow.

Pythagoras believed that numbers were divine, pure, and unchanging and that reflecting on mathematical truths could shift the psyche closer to the divine perfection of the number gods. He was concerned mainly with the symbolism of the first ten numbers (one through ten), perhaps because the Greek number system was based on ten. Others suggest the choice of ten as the limit of Pythagorean numbers is based on the fact that the numbers one, two, three, and four—which represent the four elements of the Greek universe: fire, air, water, and earth—add up to ten. It may also be that these numbers were special to Pythagoras because they were closest to one in the sacred decad one through ten. He considered one to be not only the source of all numbers but also the generative starting point of the cosmos.

Babylonian *ziggurats*, or stepped pyramids, provided a place for rituals as well as a high vantage point for astronomical observations made by the priestly class. It is thought that these structures inspired the Tibetan motif of a deity palace often placed at the center of mandalas.

We are used to thinking of numbers as abstractions, but for Pythagoras numbers were synonymous with geometric forms. One was a circle, or a single point. Two was a line between two points. Three was a triangle created by joining three points with three lines. Four was a square composed of four points connected by four lines. Five was a pentagon, six a hexagon, seven a heptagon, eight an octagon, nine a nonagon or enneagon, and ten a decagon.

Pythagoras developed a creation myth based on these numbers. He proposed that one represents unity and contains the potential for all numbers. Therefore, in the beginning, there is a single sphere of noncorporeal perfection. It is still, perfect, and complete in itself. Then the sphere of one is stimulated by a mysterious demiurge called the *Tetraktys*, which divides one into two. Two is ambivalent. It is negative in that it represents a rupture with one, the original perfection. Two is also positive, as the manifestation of potential taking form. The instability caused by the splitting of one into two sets in motion further activity that generates a third point. The three points joined with lines create a triangle, representing the number three.

Three is valued because it restores the order lost when the first perfect sphere—one—divides into two. Three also establishes the *process* that governs all matter: beginning, middle, and end. Following three, the generative process continues, and a fourth point comes into being. Connecting the four points establishes a square (four). Four signifies ordinary material reality, perhaps because it is the smallest number of surfaces that can enclose a three-dimensional space, as in a pyramid whose bottom and three sides are triangles (unlike the pyramids of Egypt that have a square base). The qualities of one, two, three, and four are considered the building blocks of all things.

Pythagoras conceptualized the cosmos as a system of concentric spheres, with the Earth in the center, analogous to the perfect sphere (one) and the five visible planets, the sun, and the moon, gracefully circling the Earth in a harmony known as the "music of the spheres." (I'll discuss the Pythagorean qualities of each number, a mixture of mathematics and philosophy, more deeply in "The Meaning behind the Numbers.")

THE GOLDEN RATIO AND FIBONACCI NUMBERS

The story goes that while tinkering with a one-stringed musical instrument with a movable fret, Pythagoras found that the sound made by plucking the string with the fret at certain places along the string was pleasing, while at other positions it was awful. He discovered that the most pleasant sounds resulted when the fret divided the string in two unequal halves where one part of the string was longer than the other part. He extrapolated this finding to his study of geometry and established the golden ratio, which is approximately 1.618034. The Pythagoreans adopted the golden ratio as the mathematical definition of beauty. When the lines and forms in a design relate to one another with the golden ratio, the design achieves desirable balance, visual harmony, and perfect form.

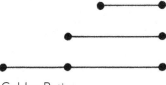

Golden Ratio:
The lesser is to the
greater as the greater is to
the sum of both.

Ideas about harmony are also found in the work of the Greek philosopher Plato. In his *Timaeus*, ca. 350 B.C.E., Plato describes the Five Platonic Solids, which are three-dimensional forms that have the same geometric shape on every face. They are named according to the number of faces they have: tetrahedron (four), cube (six), octahedron (eight), dodecahedron (twelve), and icosahedron (twenty). They represent, respectively, fire, earth, air, water, and ether. (The fifth element, ether, enabled the cosmic creator Tetraktys to set in motion cosmic creation and the orderly rhythms of stars and planets.) These forms are capable of nesting together inside a sphere, in keeping with the Pythagorean dictum that all proceeds from the sphere, or one. (See page 40 for more on the Five Platonic Solids in two dimensions.)

Drawing the solids such that they overlay each other in two dimensions produces a design known as Metatron's Cube. Metatron is an angel named in the Old Testament who served as a scribe, a sort of channel of communication. Metatron's Cube, based on a grid of thirteen spheres, is thought by some mystics to represent a "blueprint" for the creation of the cosmos. Something like the flow through the sacred Pythagorean numbers, it is thought that creation moves through the figure of Metatron's Cube in an orderly progression from one to many. (See page 40 for instructions for drawing Metatron's Cube.)

Metatron's Cube

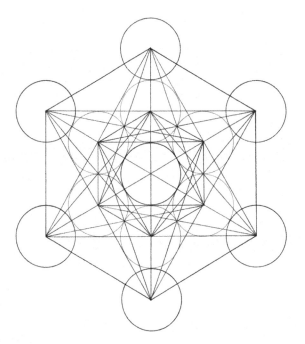

Endorsed by St. Augustine, the Pythagorean philosophy of an Earth-centric cosmos set in motion by the Prime Mover, God (or Tetraktys, in the Pythagorean system) became established Christian doctrine. The golden ratio and Pythagorean principles of sacred geometry were respected guidelines for producing sacred art and architecture in Europe. During the Middle Ages and Renaissance in Europe, artists, stonemasons, and architects aspired to align their work with classical principles of beauty, so they employed the golden ratio. The respect for Greek ideas is demonstrated by the fact that the figure of Pythagoras is even chiseled into the stone facade of Chartres Cathedral.

In his 1202 book *Liber Abaci*, an Italian mathematician named Leonardo Fibonacci introduced a numerical sequence—the Fibonacci sequence—that approximates the golden ratio. In a progression beginning with one, each number thereafter is produced by adding the two preceding numbers, a process that increases numbers by a ratio of approximately 1.6: 1, 1, 2, 3, 5, 8, 13, 21, 34, 55, 89, 144 . . . For Europeans of the era, the orderly increase of such a mathematical progression suggested the growth of living things and affirmed the orderly cycles of nature described by Pythagoras.

Interestingly, the Fibonacci sequence has been found in the natural distribution of plant seeds and leaves. For example, study of the compact arrangement of the seeds of the sunflower reveals an orderly progression of rows of smaller seeds from the center to larger seeds at the periphery in a systematic mathematical progression. The golden ratio discovered by Pythagoras in the proportions of the pentagon and five-pointed star are also present in the five-fold divisions of flowers and creatures such as starfish, sea urchins, and sand dollars. These findings affirm the intuitions of the ancient Greeks.

FROM NOTHING TO INFINITY: THE ARTFUL ZERO

Zero is notably missing from Pythagorean numbers. Pythagoras did not use a zero to write the number ten because he was not familiar with Arabic numerals; they came later. Beginning with Pythagoras and continuing well into the sixteenth century, the Western world had a problem with zero. It represented nothing, or even worse, chaos, which upset the sense of cosmic order established by the Greeks' ideas. According to St. Augustine, God was the Prime Mover who set all in motion. God, the ultimate good, could not do evil. Moreover, God could not create or coexist with nothing. Therefore, zero was judged dangerously demonic and was banished from polite discourse.

To be sure, mathematically speaking, zero does not behave as other numbers do. Adding numbers creates larger numbers and subtracting them creates smaller ones. But zero plus or minus a number leaves the number unchanged. And zero plus or minus itself is also unchanged. Even worse, zero threatens to undermine multiplication and division. Zero times any number must be zero, and when you divide by zero "all hell breaks loose."[1] The logic that binds our number system together is obliterated. Little wonder that zero was suspect for hundreds of years.

Zero was welcomed elsewhere, however. The Hindu concept of zero, or *sunya,* mentioned in Hindu texts from the sixth to eighth centuries C.E., was associated with the pregnant void, full of potential, from which all creation streams. According to the Rig Veda: "In the earliest age of the gods, existence was born from non-existence."[2]

In the South Asian tradition, zero was associated with creative potential and infinite possibilities. As the Indian numbering system made its way to Europe via the Arabian Peninsula, zero traveled with it. Passed along through northern Africa, then to Spain and Italy, zero followed the southern route to Europe, carried by traders and the commerce they generated, arriving by 970 C.E., or possibly even a hundred years earlier. Interestingly, zero even found its way, briefly, into Christian religious thought.

During the early 1300s in Germany, the Dominican mystic Meister Eckhart, flirting with heresy, taught that

> being empty of things is to be full of God; that God, who must lie past all knowledge and all Being, must therefore also be nothing. . . . God and I are One. Now I am what I was and I neither add to nor subtract from anything.[3]

This is the very definition of zero. While heretical for Christianity, Islam, rooted in Eastern thought, had no problem accepting zero. Muslim philosophy taught that God created the cosmos from the void. Muslims embraced the void—and also the numbers of Pythagoras.

THE SACRED ART OF ISLAM

The sages of Islam found that the ideas of Pythagoras could be easily assimilated into their own beliefs:

> The Pythagorean philosophy of mathematics provided the language and presented an already elaborated science, itself of an esoteric nature and going back to Egypt and Babylon, for the "spiritual mathematic" which is so central to Islamic [art and] architecture.[4]

The Islamic dictum that "there is no God but God" means that God is the unity from which all things flow. God is the eternal source and basis of all. The material world is thought to be transitory and illusory. Emptiness, the void, is a metaphor for the all-encompassing unity of God. This belief is expressed by designs where careful attention is given to the negative spaces around lines and forms, especially in calligraphy. And so zero, representing emptiness or the void, can be the ultimate expression of sacred geometry.

Islamic tile work designs typically include pointed stars and arrowhead shapes suggesting energy projecting outward, along with petal-like shapes such as unequal hexagrams suggesting energy flowing inward. The result is a balance between centripetal and centrifugal force that illuminates the Islamic principle of unity as a balance of opposites.

Attunement to God is necessary for an Islamic artist, for when he or she takes pen in hand, the artist becomes an instrument of God.

The Arabic mathematical term *al-jabr*, which refers to a process of calculation, is thought to be the root of the word *algebra*.

Islamic Design

The geometric designs of Islam are crafted with great care. The practice is contemplative, and the designs convey a sense of reverence. The art created with such devotion is considered a spiritual beacon for the community.

The role of zero in creating mandalas is overtly obvious in that both zeros and mandalas are circles. A mandala circle can bring together seemingly contradictory meanings. For example, it can be full (as the moon) and empty (as a cave). It can signify something very small (atoms) and something quite large (our solar system), even representing both at the same time. And so the mandala circle can act as a bridge from our innermost personal experience to the vastness of the universe, helping us feel at home among the circling stars.

NUMBERS IN JEWISH MYSTICISM

In Judaism a belief in the mystical powers of numbers was part of the scholarly tradition for reading the creation story in the Hebrew Bible. Then, during the Middle Ages, interest in new forms of mysticism arose.

Maimonides, a twelfth-century rabbi, found a way to resolve the prevailing European abhorrence for zero and the void. He agreed with St. Augustine that God was indeed the creator of the universe, but, he pointed out, the God of the Old Testament created the universe from *nothing*. He thereby moved the void from sacrilege to sacredness. His teaching paved the way for the development of Kabbalah.

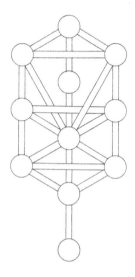

Kabbalah Tree of Life

With the appearance of the Zohar in the thirteenth century C.E., the study of Kabbalah gained great popularity. Kabbalah teaches of the ten *sephiroth,* or divine emanations, which are the mysterious unfolding of God in the world. God, the *Ein Sof* (Infinite One), manifests his divine existence through the flow of these ten emanations. The diagram of the sephiroth is known as the Tree of Life. The design known as the Flower of Life provides the structure for the Tree of Life. (See page 39 for drawing instructions.) The first sephirah is called Keter (Crown). The others appear in this order: Hokhmah (Wisdom), Binah (Intelligence), Hesed (Mercy), Din (Judgment) or Gevurah (Strength), Tiferet (Beauty), Netzah (Victory), Hod (Splendor), Yesod (Foundation), and Malkhut (Kingdom).

Kabbalah, to this day, is an important thread in the tapestry of Judaism. Another mystical thread in that faith that is also mentioned in the Zohar is Metatron, the angelic being associated with Metatron's Cube described above. (See page 40 for drawing instructions.)

JUNG, MANDALAS, AND PYTHAGOREAN NUMBERS

C. G. Jung was aware of the philosophy of Pythagoras regarding the monad, or "one as source," and found it helpful in formulating his own inner experience that culminated in the creation of mandalas:

> I had the distinct feeling that [the mandalas] were something
> central, and in time I acquired through them a living conception
> of the Self. The Self, I thought, was like the monad which I am,
> and which is my world. The mandala represents this monad,
> and corresponds to the microcosmic nature of the psyche.[5]

"In all mandalas in which numbers are the predominant element, it is number symbolism which can best plumb its meaning."[6]

Jung, like Pythagoras, emphasizes the importance of the numbers one through four in his psychology. For Jung, one signifies original wholeness. Two relates to the psyche's split between conscious and unconscious, self and nonself, and other intractable conflicts. Three is the bridging of this split by a third entity—the ego, which is the center of consciousness. Four manifests with the conscious realization by the ego of the Self, an unconscious center that functions as the true center of the psyche. The Self is the matrix that births and maintains the ego. Only when the ego comes to terms with the fact that it is not the center of the psyche is wholeness possible. It is the Self that generates an urge to create mandalas as an expression of an individual's wholeness.

Jung posited that the psyche uses four functions—thinking, feeling, sensing, and intuiting—as modes for gathering information about the world. Reliance on all four is ideal. Pythagoras also saw the number four as symbolic of the psyche, although he believed the four elements were earth, fire, air, and water. Jung espoused the Pythagorean conception that progress takes place when conflict between two opposites generates a third element that subsumes the opposites and establishes harmony.

Jung applied this Pythagorean numbering system to the interpretation of mandalas. Mandalas with no divisions suggest a beginner's mind. When divided in two, conflict that generates energy for growth is present. A mandala with three divisions reveals activity to resolve conflict in a new synthesis, and one with four parts reveals a balance in the use of the four functions and harmony in the relationship between ego and Self. This is the Jungian definition of wholeness.

Once thought of as esoteric knowledge, numbers operate in ways that are amazing even by today's secular standards. For example, consider this beautiful array of numbers that arises from simply multiplying the number one by itself, subsequently appending the number one to each factor and multiplying again, and so on, nine times as shown here:

$1 \times 1 = 1$
$11 \times 11 = 121$
$111 \times 111 = 12321$
$1111 \times 1111 = 1234321$
$11111 \times 11111 = 123454321$
$111111 \times 111111 = 12345654321$
$1111111 \times 1111111 = 1234567654321$
$11111111 \times 11111111 = 123456787654321$
$111111111 \times 111111111 = 12345678987654321$

What are we to make of such an orderly flow of numbers? Does it bolster the claim of Pythagoras that all numbers derive from the number one? Could it be proof of a deep ordering principal at work, possibly even God? Is this simply more evidence that numbers are coincidental?

Or is number sense embedded in our organism? We know, for example, that babies as young as five months old can distinguish between two and three dots even without any knowledge of numbers or the ability to count. And our preference for base-ten numbering systems no doubt has something to do with the fact that we have two hands with five fingers each. While these points are certainly relevant, let us consider another possible explanation for the profundity of numbers.

Toward the end of his vast exploration of the human psyche, Jung came to the understanding that all of nature, including human beings, is structured by ordering principles he called "archetypes." We are usually not aware of archetypes, yet they exert influence and generate meaningful experiences for us. Also, the actions taken by people activate, or set in motion, the energy of an archetype. As Richard Tarnas explains, archetypes function as "autonomous patterns of meaning that appear to structure and inhere in both psyche and matter."[7]

This suggests that our reality has an already existing order and that this order affects our attempts to know it. We cannot look at things from *outside* this natural structure of meaning. In fact, it has been found by scientists that the very act of looking changes what we are looking at. Simply put, there is no separation between subject and object. As James Hillman states:

> The evidence we gather in support of a hypothesis and the rhetoric we use to argue it are already part of the archetypal constellation we are in. . . . The "objective" idea we find in the pattern of data is also the "subjective" idea by means of which we see the data.[8]

This archetypal structure both makes possible and limits knowing, whether it's of an infant or Einstein. The sublime notion of sacred geometry might be our glimpse of this underlying archetypal order. And our amazing findings about the beauty and elegance of numbers could be produced by the same archetypal ground. As M. L. von Franz explains, numbers "may well be the most primitive element of order in the human mind. . . . Thus we define number psychologically as an archetype of order which has become conscious."[9]

Is it any wonder that this quest leads us back to an appreciation that we are, and always have been, deeply embedded in the flux and flow of natural cycles? Our ancestors sought to align themselves with the natural forces of the cosmos by creating images of the sun and moon. Later, they studied and described the cycles of nature with numbers, geometry, and mathematics. They have given us the opportunity to continue the dance of evolution through our own creative self-expression and to discover for ourselves the "archetype of order which has become conscious." It feels good to be in harmony with nature's order. But is this order God? I leave that to you to decide.

Numbers have been used for thousands of years in religious practices. They have been revered as something divine, orderly, and numinous. The knowledge of numbers, geometry, and mathematics has endowed people with god-like abilities to construct things of awesome power and beauty. Let us now claim our opportunity to use the knowledge of numbers for our own personal quest for meaning.

THE MEANING
BEHIND THE NUMBERS

IN THE ANCIENT PHILOSOPHY of Pythagoras, numbers are revered as sacred geometric forms. These numbers/forms are thought to be the foundation of all that is—the very building blocks of matter. The numerical/geometrical flow from one to ten signifies the process of orderly natural growth by which everything comes into being. This antique number philosophy is beautiful, prescientific, and powerful. It influences our thinking even today. (See pages 5–11 for more about Pythagorean numbers.)

In addition to the Pythagorean numbers, I include the numbers eleven, twelve, and thirteen. Their traditional meanings and graphic representations are also important in the history of sacred geometry. Eleven is esteemed as a double one by some sacred geometers, twelve is an archetypal number associated with the passage of time, and thirteen is significant in labyrinth symbolism. All the mandalas in this book are based on the geometric forms associated with the numbers one through thirteen.

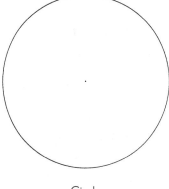

Circle

THIS BELONGS TO ONE

One is a circle, the epitome of unity and stillness, complete and perfect in itself. (See page 44 for drawing instructions.) One is orderly and stands

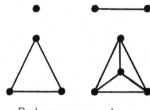

Pythagorean numbers
one through four

alone against the chaos of no limits, such as zero or infinity. Pythagoras taught that all that is good in the universe comes from one. In the words of his devotee Iamblichus (ca. 250–330 C.E.):

> Everything has been organized by the monad [one], because it contains everything potentially: for even if they are not yet actual, nevertheless the monad holds seminally the principles which are within all numbers.[1]

In terms of geometry, one is a point that connotes position but cannot represent direction, surface, or content. Nevertheless, one has unique mathematical properties. Any number multiplied by 1 is itself, the same. For instance, $3 \times 1 = 3$ and $4 \times 1 = 4$. And, of course, $1 \times 1 = 1$. This perhaps explains why Pythagoras thought of one as the support of all other numbers, and one is the source of all *odd* numbers. Pythagoras considered one masculine, referred to it as the "monad," and associated it with fire, the sun, or the central hearth of home. One is also identified with either Apollo (the solar god) or Zeus (the father of the gods, creator of the cosmos).

TWO ESTABLISHES EITHER/OR

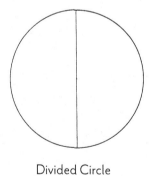

Divided Circle

Two is a circle divided by a line into equal halves. (See page 45 for drawing instructions.) Two establishes duality and introduces the possibility of *either/or*, the world of opposites. For Pythagoras this is both good and bad. He considers two impulsive for leaving the eternal stability of one and generating the material world with all its woes. Yet he also considers the cosmos a harmonious balance of opposites, which is only made possible by the division of two from one. It follows that two represents both rivalry and mutual dependence. Two is special because it is closer to one in the numbering order than any other number. It stands as an important bridge between one and three.

With two, one can measure distance, direction, beginning, and end. Two makes possible division of numbers into even and odd. Two is the first prime number, which means it can only be divided evenly by one or itself. The specialness of two can be further demonstrated mathematically. When adding or multiplying two by itself, we get the same result: $2 + 2 = 4$ and $2 \times 2 = 4$. Two is the *only* positive whole number that gives the same outcome when added to or multiplied by itself. For numbers three and above, multiplying numbers by themselves yields numbers *larger* than adding numbers to themselves. By contrast, multiplying one by itself yields a number *smaller* than adding it to itself: $1 \times 1 = 1$, while $1 + 1 = 2$.

For Pythagoras, two is the opposite of one in every way. It is associated with matter, which is always in a state of flux, and with the moon, with its varying halves of dark and light. Two is an *even* number and, as the designated opposite of one, it is considered female. Two has to do with sex as well, and Pythagoras credits two with attracting one to create three.

A radius is the distance from the center of a circle to any point on the circle. A polygon is a two-dimensional closed shape formed with straight lines.

THREE IS A TRIANGLE

Three repairs the rupture caused when two splits from one, by generating a new synthesis that does not eliminate the duality but incorporates it into a new pattern, like a child who brings parents together and forms a family. Three is also equated with marriage because it is created by the merger of one (masculine) and two (feminine), for $1 + 2 = 3$. Unlike two, which is associated with contrast, opposition, and either/or, three relates to friendship, peace, and harmony. Three symbolizes the energy of *becoming*, of taking form. It is "by tradition symbolic of human consciousness."[2] Prayers, mantras, and benedictions are customarily

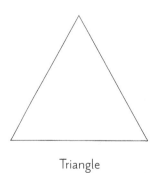

Triangle

repeated three times to evoke the generative harmony of three, and you have no doubt heard that the "third time is a charm."

To Pythagoras, three is the first real number because with three points and three lines one can establish the simplest possible polygon: a triangle. In fact, all polygons can be reduced to a triangle. (See page 46 for drawing instructions.) Three, like two, is a prime number. It is associated with natural processes. It incorporates the qualities of one (unity) with two (beginning/ending) and becomes the beginning, middle, and ending—a complete process. Three is associated with wisdom, for the Pythagoreans believed a wise person acts appropriately in the present by factoring in knowledge gained from past experiences and looking ahead to future consequences.

Square

FOUR IS A SQUARE

The number four possesses more symbolism than any of the other deified Pythagorean numbers, one through ten. Four, represented as a square, is regarded as a key to the natural world and physical experiences. (See page 50 for drawing instructions.) It represents the world with its four cardinal directions (north, east, south, west), four elements (fire, air, water, earth), four winds, and four seasons, as well as the four parts of the body (head, trunk, legs, arms). It also represents the human psyche.

The Pythagoreans thought of four as a ten in disguise.[3] This is because the sum of the first four numbers equals ten (1 + 2 + 3 + 4 = 10). As a symbol of this important concept, Pythagoreans laid out ten points forming a triangle (see page 27). Through four, the creative potential of the numbers one through three flows into embodiment in the physical realm as the numbers five, six, seven, eight, nine, and ten. Four is also a symbol of the demiurge, or Tetraktys, that works through numbers one through ten to bring the cosmos into being.

FIVE IS FAVORED

The geometric figure associated with five is the pentagon. (See page 54 for drawing instructions.) Connecting the points of a pentagon with diagonals generates a five-pointed star, also known as a pentacle. The length of each diagonal is approximately 1.6 times longer than a side of the pentagon, a relationship known as the golden ratio. One can create a five-pointed star by measuring five angles of 72 degrees each in a circle and then connecting the points across the circle. Adding to the mystique of the number five is the fact that the number of degrees to construct it, 72, is itself a potent talisman. It is divisible by all the numbers one through nine, except five and the number seven. Seventy-two is significant in number lore for its relation to twelve, the basis of the zodiac: it is divisible by twelve, two, three, and six.

For Pythagoras, five represented the body: its trunk, two arms, and two legs. Five also represented the five planets known to him (Mercury, Venus, Mars, Saturn, and Jupiter). Five is sometimes called "marriage"

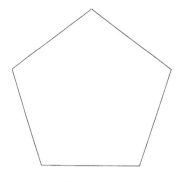

Pentagon

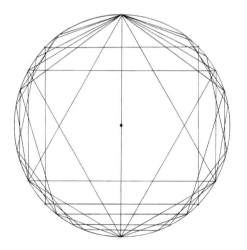

1 2 3 4 5 6 7 8 9 10

This mandala illustrates all of the geometric forms associated with the Pythagorean numbers 1 through 10: circle, semicircle, triangle, square, pentagon, hexagon, octagon, nonagon, and decagon.

since it is the combination of an even (female) and an odd (male) number (2 + 3 = 5). As such it is sacred to the goddess Aphrodite, who governs love relationships. Five is a prime number and near the center in the number series one through ten. This pivotal placement of five might have reminded the Greeks of a scale, with five serving as the fulcrum balancing the numbers on either side of it. The Pythagoreans associate five with justice. Also, because of its position in the middle, five signifies moderation.

Five has interesting mathematical attributes. It is a "circular number," meaning that the product of multiplying it by itself always ends in five. For instance, 5 cubed = 125. Five also claims "primary perfection" in that the last two digits of its cube (125) repeat its square (25). Furthermore, five is not the product of any two other numbers in the one-through-ten sequence, although five can generate ten, as in 2 × 5 = 10.

SIX IS BEAUTIFUL

Six has mathematical properties that endeared it to ancient philosophers. Six is the first "perfect number," which means that its factors (not including itself) add up to itself: 1 + 2 + 3 = 6. Another notable feature is that when multiplied, its factors (not including itself) also result in six: 6 × 1 = 6, 2 × 3 = 6. Like five, six is also a circular number, so when it is squared and cubed, the results end in six: 6 cubed = 216. The distinctiveness of six is further justified by mathematical operations that reveal its numerous hidden groupings of three that resolve neatly into six. We can see how this is possible by dividing the numbers one through nine into groupings of three digits, and adding the numbers in each grouping, as follows:

1 + 2 + 3 = 6
4 + 5 + 6 = 15, and 1 + 5 = 6
7 + 8 + 9 = 24, and 2 + 4 = 6

Six is represented by a hexagon. It is also related to the ancient geometric pattern called the Flower of Life. With only a compass, a systematic grid based on a six-petaled flower can be generated. (See page 58 for drawing instructions.) A variation is the mandala comprised of six circles surrounding a center circle of the same size, which later took on significance in Christian and Islamic faiths as the six days of creation with the center circle representing the seventh day of rest. Such grids underlie many designs in sacred geometry, including the Five Platonic Solids, Metatron's Cube, and the Kabbalah Tree of Life.

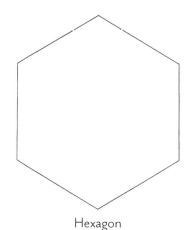

Hexagon

The hexagon is a natural division of a circle because each side of the hexagon is equal to the radius of the circle that encloses it. This links six with the Pythagorean one, symbolized by a circle. Finding so many interesting geometric and mathematical operations related to six deeply impressed the ancient Greeks. For them six meant stability, wholeness, and beauty.

SEVEN STANDS ALONE

Seven is represented by a seven-sided polygon, or heptagon. (See page 62 for drawing instructions.) Seven is important for the fact that seven heavenly bodies (sun, moon, Mercury, Mars, Venus, Jupiter, and Saturn) comprised the orderly known universe of the Greeks. Seven symbolizes growth because its factors are three (process) and four (matter). Ancients believed that most seeds sprouted within seven days. Pythagoras called seven a "crisis," and considered days divisible by seven, such as the seventh, fourteenth, and twenty-eighth days of the month, to be pivotal times.

Heptagon

Seven, as a prime number, was an anomaly for the Greeks. It cannot be added to or multiplied by any of the numbers one through ten and produce a number that occurs in this desirable range. The Pythagoreans expressed this metaphorically by saying that seven cannot be produced by "intercourse" of any of the numbers one though ten. Furthermore, it

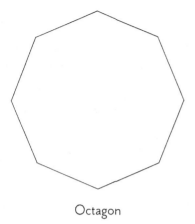

Octagon

is difficult to create a geometric figure based on its number. Because it is unable to join harmoniously with other numbers, seven is called "virgin" and symbolizes the virgin goddess Athena. And since Athena was born from the head of Zeus, seven also represents the mind.

EIGHT IS LOVING

The octagon signifies the number eight. (See page 66 for drawing instructions.) Because of the harmony of its parts (a doubling of four, which is the basic building block of the cosmos), Pythagoreans associate eight with love, friendship, wisdom, and creative thought. It also represents the cosmic realm of the fixed stars outside the seven planetary spheres. Eight is notable as the first mathematical cube ($8 = 2 \times 2 \times 2$) and is valued because it is simpler, closer to one, and therefore more godly than the next cube, twenty-seven ($27 = 3 \times 3 \times 3$). In a final example of eight's mathematical harmony, the square of every odd number above one is a multiple of eight plus one: 5 squared $= 25 = (3 \times 8) + 1$.

NINE HOLDS THE LINE

Nonagon

Nine is the next-to-last number of the deified Pythagorean decade. It is represented by a nonagon or enneagon. (See page 70 or drawing instructions.) Pythagoras considered it a boundary that held other numbers in order. Nine puts a stop to the unfolding of cosmic creation rippling through the numbers one through eight, thereby protecting the cosmos from unbridled generativity, which, according to Pythagorean beliefs, would lead to the horror of infinite chaos. Nine accomplishes this service by containing within itself several threes, which symbolize process. Both addition and multiplication of threes produce nine: $3 + 3 + 3 = 9$ and $3 \times 3 = 9$. Also, *any* number multiplied by nine results in a number whose numerals added together result in nine: $5 \times 9 = 45$, and $4 + 5 = 9$.

TEN EMBRACES EVERYTHING

Ten is represented by a decagon, a ten-sided polygon. When a decagon is drawn inside a circle, the decagon takes up most of the space inside the circle. (See page 74 for drawing instructions.) Perhaps this is why Pythagoras referred to ten as "all-embracing, all-limiting mother."[4] Ten signifies completion, balance, and wholeness.

As the sum of the first four numbers (1 + 2 + 3 + 4 = 10), ten is also associated with the meaning of all its constituent numbers: primordial existence signified by one, duality as shown in two, lively process associated with three, and solidity as seen in four. Ten, when represented in a triangular arrangement of ten points, also symbolizes the creative demiurge, Tetraktys, revered by Pythagoreans. So, according to Pythagoras, ten contains everything.

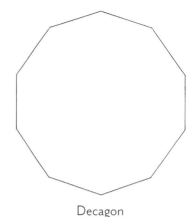

Decagon

Pythagorean Pyramid

BEYOND PYTHAGORAS: ELEVEN, TWELVE, AND THIRTEEN

Pythagorean tradition permeates the philosophy of the numbers one through ten. Of course, number symbolism is not solely the purview of Pythagoras. Yet, it is hard to know how many numbers to include. Twelve is such a powerful symbolic number it simply cannot be left out of a book on sacred geometry. Thirteen is important because of its association with

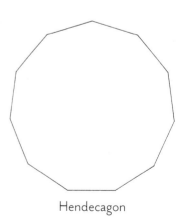

Hendecagon

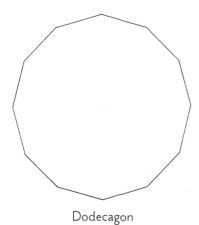

Dodecagon

A Pythagorean oath states: "I swear it by him who into our souls has transmitted the Sacred Quaternary [Tetraktys]."[5]

the labyrinth. Eleven should then be included largely because it is *on the way* to twelve and thirteen in the numbering sequence. Nonetheless, eleven has qualities that make it interesting as well.

An eleven-sided polygon is called a hendecagon. (See page 78 for drawing instructions.) Eleven, coming after ten, the Pythagorean number of perfection, suffers by comparison. It is a symbol of excess, peril, conflict, and martyrdom. Surprisingly, it can also be considered like a Pythagorean two because it is made up of two ones, as in 1 + 1 = 2. Therefore, the Pythagorean two's qualities of disruption, yet generativity, can be applied to eleven as well. Could this ambivalent quality of eleven have influenced the builders of the Chartres Cathedral labyrinth to use eleven concentric circles as the pathway to and from the center?

A twelve-sided polygon is known as a dodecagon. (See page 82 for drawing instructions.) Twelve represents a complete cycle, cosmic order, and wholeness. There are twelve signs of the zodiac, twelve months of the year, twelve hours of day and night. The twelfth day following the winter solstice marked the beginning of the Roman Saturnalia. The quality of each day was thought to presage the twelve months of the upcoming year. The twelve days of Christmas that begin on Christmas Day were once thought to make similar predictions for the year. There are twelve tribes of Israel, twelve Knights of the Round Table, and prior to the modern era the Dalai Lama held a circular council comprised of twelve advisers.

The number twelve holds within it the Pythagorean numbers for the four elements: fire (one), air (two), water (three), and earth (four). Its factors, three and four, make twelve an important point of cosmic balance. Three is associated with dynamism or inner spirituality, while four connotes stability or outer activity. When three and four, the factors of twelve, are added, the result is the prime number seven. This result adds significance to three and four, which in turn imbues their product, twelve, with more clout.

We are accustomed to using a numbering system based on ten, but it is also possible to have a system based on twelve, or even sixty. The ancient Babylonians used such numbering systems. Twelve as a basis of numbering imbued that number with profound sacred meaning. Vestiges of Babylonian numbering are revealed in our use of twelve and sixty for reckoning time and for fundamental operations in geometry. (Sixty minutes make an hour, twelve hours make a day, and 360 degrees divided by six is sixty.)

Twelve is closely associated with the circle. In fact, a polygon with twelve sides, a dodecagon, is almost a circle. (See page 82 for instructions for drawing.) Cirlot asserts that "systems or patterns based upon the circle or the cycle tend to have 12 as the end-limit."[6] This certainly holds true for the labyrinth at Chartres because the eleven circuits of the pathway culminate at the center, the twelfth and final circle.

A thirteen-sided polygon is called a tridecagon. (See page 86 for drawing instructions.) Thirteen is traditionally considered an unlucky number. Some count the traitor Judas as the thirteenth, set apart from the sanctified twelve (Jesus and his eleven loyal disciples). However, thirteen appears in the Old Testament as the number of salvation. In base-twelve numbering systems, thirteen is thought to bring good fortune, though for the Babylonians, thirteen was the number of the underworld and signified destruction of perfection. Elsewhere in antiquity, thirteen was a symbol of strength and the sublime. For example, Zeus was sometimes described as the thirteenth in the circle of the twelve chief gods. Cirlot summarizes the meaning of thirteen as "symbolic of death and birth, of beginning afresh."[7]

Thirteen is a prime number. Some Greeks saw it as an expression of the Prime Mover, or God. All the star mandalas derived from a thirteen-pointed tridecagon can be created by a single line. (See Tridecagons, pages 88–89.) Stars such as these are traditionally associated with spiritual protection. Could this explain why the Chartres Cathedral labyrinth is based on an invisible thirteen-pointed star? Lauren Artress believes

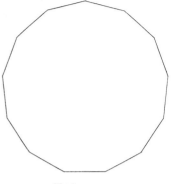

Tridecagon

that "the invisible star empowers the [Chartres] labyrinth."[8] Perhaps the builders of the labyrinth utilized the star as a way of bringing the vitality and sanctuary of the Prime Mover into their construction.

The symbolism of numbers is rich, complex, and fascinating. This brief description of the meaning of numbers and forms in sacred geometry provides an introductory sampling. Knowing these traditional number meanings and the geometric forms associated with them will inspire enjoyable new (and old!) ways of creating mandalas.

TECHNIQUES AND
PRINCIPLES FOR DRAWING

MANDALAS CREATED with sacred geometry can be spontaneously fash-
ioned out of materials conveniently close at hand, or they can be carefully
measured and drawn constructions where each line has special meaning
for the artist, even when it cannot be seen in the finished mandala. These
two are not mutually exclusive; you might set out with a predetermined
plan for a geometric mandala and along the way be led by your intuition
to add something unplanned for reasons unknown.

The process of drawing a mandala with geometry is often medita-
tive. Once decisions are made about the design, creating the mandala
becomes a rhythmic repetition of smooth, sure lines, intriguing conver-
gences, and gratifying results. Moreover, even when it's carefully con-
structed, a mandala takes on significance for its creator beyond being a
mere drawing exercise.

Drawing mandalas with sacred geometry requires special equipment. In addition to paper and pencils you will need a straightedge or
ruler, a compass, a protractor, and an eraser. A compass allows you to
draw circles of the size you wish. Those with a screw adjustment are the
most reliable. A protractor measures degrees (a circle has 360 degrees)
and it allows you to determine angles, which can provide a useful shortcut when drawing some mandalas. The triangles can be aligned to draw

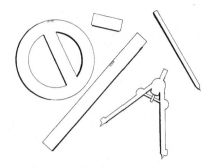

lines parallel to each other, to establish a 90-degree angle, and even serve as a straightedge in a pinch. Drafting tape can be used to keep your paper from moving when you are drawing.

Other optional equipment that you may find useful includes a plastic circle template, a compass that holds an ink pen, and a compass extension arm for drawing large circles. I typically have several compasses that I leave set for drawing different-sized circles to avoid tedious adjustments.

EQUIPMENT

Paper, 8½" × 11" or larger

Pencil, erasable lead

Pencils, assorted colors

Pens for drafting, drawing, and coloring

Eraser (soft)

Straightedge or ruler

Compass

Protractor, 360-degree circular

Two 90-degree (right) triangles

Drafting tape

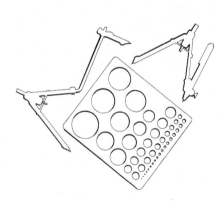

OPTIONAL EQUIPMENT

Circle template

Ink pen compass

Extendable compass

HOW TO BEGIN

Secure your drawing paper with small pieces of drafting tape at each corner. I suggest that you draw your mandala design first in pencil, then go over your pencil lines with ink. When the ink is dry, you can erase your pencil lines for a crisp, clean result. Then you can add color. Or, if you like, you can omit the inking step and proceed directly to adding color with pencils, markers, or other media of your choice.

Establish the center of your piece of paper by extending a straight-edge from the top left corner to the bottom right corner. Using your lead drawing pencil, draw a line against the straightedge two or three inches long near the center of the paper. Repeat this step from the upper right to the lower left corners. You will have an *X* that marks the center of your paper. Adjust your compass for the size of mandala you wish to draw. Place the sharp point of your compass on the center point of your paper and scribe a complete circle (see Beginning 1).

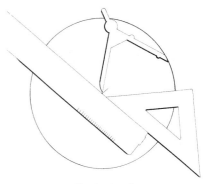

Beginning 1

Draw a vertical line through the center of your circle (O) that is per-pendicular (90 degrees) to the bottom edge of your paper. Establishing this line in the circle provides a useful starting point for the design of your mandala. To do so, place a right (90 degree) triangle so that one short side lines up with the bottom edge of the paper, and the other short side touches the center of your circle. Using your triangle as a straightedge, draw a straight line from the top to the bottom of the circle (see Beginning 2). This line should pass through the center of the circle.

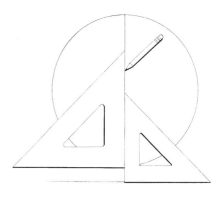

Beginning 2

To find a second line intersecting the circle horizontally, adjust your compass to one inch *larger* than for your original circle. Place the point where the line intersects the top of the circle and draw arcs on the right and left sides inside the circle. Then place your compass point at the bottom of the circle where the line intersects it and scribe arcs to intersect those just drawn. Using a straightedge, create a line through the center point of the circle and arc intersections on both sides of the circle. Your circle is now divided into four equal parts.

Using these steps to begin drawing the mandalas in this book will ensure that your mandala will be centered on your paper.

USING A PROTRACTOR

If you prefer, you can use your protractor to find the points for the horizontal line by following these steps. With your circle centered, drawn, and bisected by a line perpendicular to the bottom of your paper, place the protractor in the center of your circle with 0 degrees at the top and

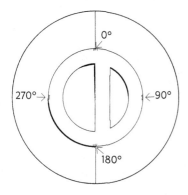

Protractor 1

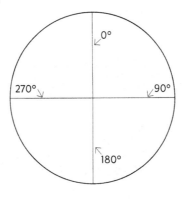

Protractor 2

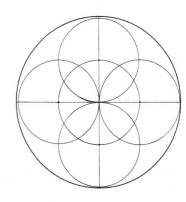

Protractor 3

180 degrees at the bottom, both aligned with the perpendicular line running through your circle. The center mark of the protractor should be on top of the center point of your circle (see Protractor 1). Mark with your pencil the protractor points at 90 degrees and 270 degrees. Draw a line connecting these two points. You now have a circle divided into four equal parts (see Protractor 2).

Along one of the lines, measure and mark half the distance between the center and the edge of the circle. Set your compass to this distance. Place the point of your compass at the center of your circle and scribe a circle. Then place your compass point at each place where lines intersect the circle you just drew, and scribe a circle (see Protractor 3). You have created a mandala with sacred geometry.

To draw a square, prepare your drawing as described above, with your circle centered, drawn, and bisected by a line perpendicular to the bottom of your paper. Place the protractor in the center of your circle with 0 degrees at the top and 180 degrees at the bottom, both aligned with the perpendicular line running through your circle. The center mark of the protractor should be on top of the center point of your circle. Find and mark points at 45 degrees, 135 degrees, 225 degrees, and 315 degrees (see

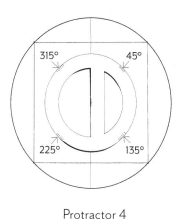

Protractor 4

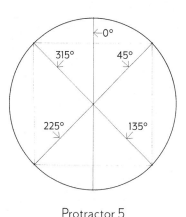

Protractor 5

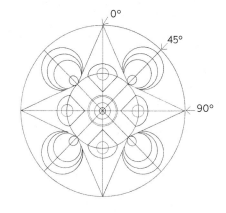

Protractor 6

Protractor 4). Remove the protractor and use your straightedge to draw lines connecting the points you just marked with the protractor. The lines should intersect the center of your circle. Now connect the points where these two lines intersect the circle (see Protractor 5). You will have drawn a square.

These steps are the foundation for more complex designs. For example, the steps described above are used for establishing the matrix for the mandala shown (see Protractor 6). A circle template is also useful in constructing this mandala. Place a circle template precisely along lines of the mandala matrix, and trace a circle, being careful to keep pen or pencil vertical to your paper to ensure a well-rounded circle.

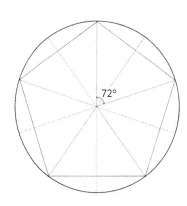

Protractor 7

The same technique described above for measuring angles with a protractor can be used to create a pentagon. Prepare your drawing as you did for the square. With your protractor aligned with the vertical line running through your circle, mark the points for the pentagon at 72 degrees, 144 degrees, 216 degrees, and 288 degrees. Use your straightedge to connect the lines through the center of your circle and intersect the circle (see Protractor 7). Now connect every other point that intersects the circle. Other figures can be created inside a circle in the same way. Here is a summary of the figures and the angles to establish them:

Divide circle in half . . . . 180 degrees

Triangle (three sides) . . . . 120 degrees

Square (four sides) . . . . 90 degrees

Pentagon (five sides) . . . . 72 degrees

Hexagon (six sides) . . . . 60 degrees

Heptagon (seven sides) . . . . 51.4 degrees

Octagon (eight sides) . . . . 45 degrees

Nonagon or Enneagon (nine sides) . . . . 40 degrees

Decagon (ten sides) . . . . 36 degrees

Hendecagon (eleven sides) . . . . 32.5 degrees

Dodecagon (twelve sides) . . . . 30 degrees

Tridecagon (thirteen sides) . . . . 27.7 degrees

CREATING A BASIC MANDALA GRID

To draw symmetrical mandala designs, it's helpful to set up a foundation as your guide. First, create a circle divided into eighteen segments by measuring angles of 20 degrees (see Mandala Grid 1). Next,

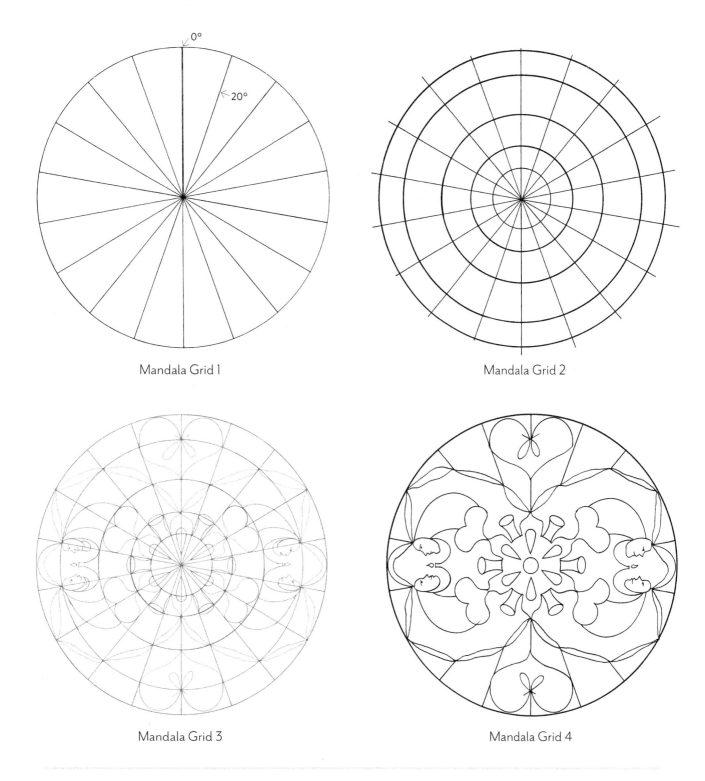

Mandala Grid 1

Mandala Grid 2

Mandala Grid 3

Mandala Grid 4

adjust your compass to a radius approximately one inch smaller than the original circle. Place your compass point at the center of the circle and draw a circle. Continue this way until you have drawn four circles, each smaller than the last (see Mandala Grid 2). You now have a basic mandala grid that is useful for creating mandalas with a symmetrical design. Mandala Grids 3 and 4 illustrate a mandala drawing in progress using the grid and the completed mandala ready for coloring.

USING CIRCLES TO CREATE A MANDALA GRID

Before the invention of the protractor in the late 1500s, grids of overlapping circles of the same size provided a structure for designs both large and small. A circle template is convenient for establishing such a grid. The Flower of Life (see Using Circles 2) is an example of using circles as the basis for a larger design such as Metatron's Cube (see page 40) and many other sacred designs and patterns. The Tree of Life, a design illustrating

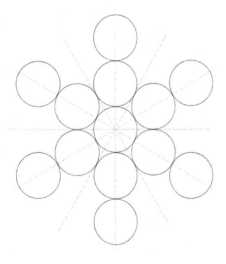

Using Circles 1

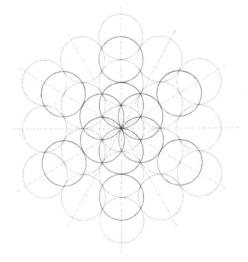

Using Circles 2

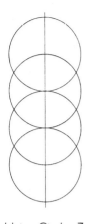

Using Circles 3

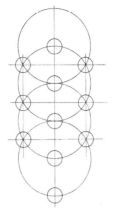

Using Circles 4

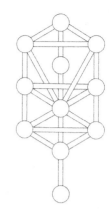

Using Circles 5

the emanations of God, is important in Kabbalah. The progression of this design begins with a grid of overlapping circles (see Using Circles 2, 3, and 4), which provides a structure for recreating this sacred design.

Using Circles 6

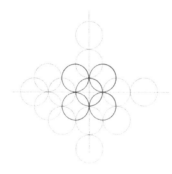

Using Circles 7

Using Circles 8

There are many variations on circular grids. I used a grid of circles to develop a version of the Sri Yantra mandala (see Using Circles 6). First I established a grid of circles (see Using Circles 7), and then I used that grid to draw the Sri Yantra mandala (see Using Circles 8).

METATRON'S CUBE AND FIVE PLATONIC SOLIDS

Metatron's Cube is a drawing based on a grid of circles that incorporates the Five Platonic Solids drawn in two dimensions (see Metatron's Cube). Here is a shortcut to drawing Metatron's Cube: create the Flower of Life grid marking the centers of all circles (see Metatron's Cube 1). Then simply connect *each* center point to *every other* center point with straight lines to create a tetrahedron, or pyramid, with four sides (see Metatron's Cube 2); a cube with six sides (see Metatron's Cube 3), an octahedron with eight sides (see Metatron's Cube 4), a dodecahedron with twelve sides (see Metatron's Cube 5), and an icosahedron with twenty sides (see Metatron's Cube 6).

This mandala (Metatron's Cube 7) illustrates the notion of ancient geometry that *all* is composed of squares and triangles. In this twelve-sided figure, the three-dimensional Platonic Solid of the octahedron is emphasized with dark lines.

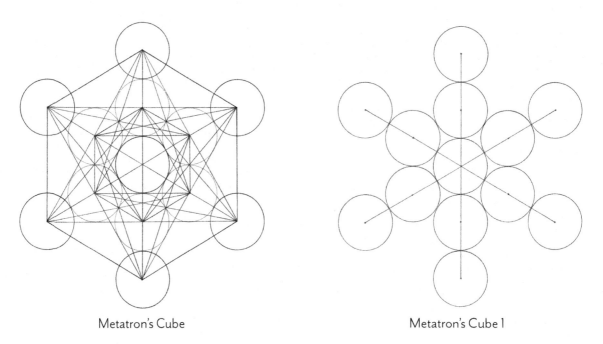

Metatron's Cube   Metatron's Cube 1

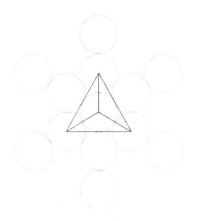

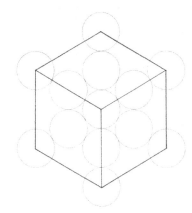

Left: Metatron's Cube 2
Right: Metatron's Cube 3

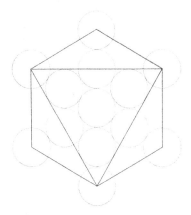

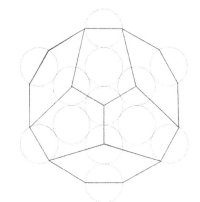

Left: Metatron's Cube 4
Right: Metatron's Cube 5

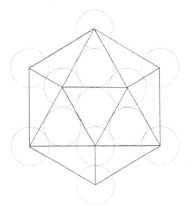

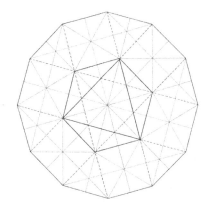

Left: Metatron's Cube 6
Right: Metatron's Cube 7

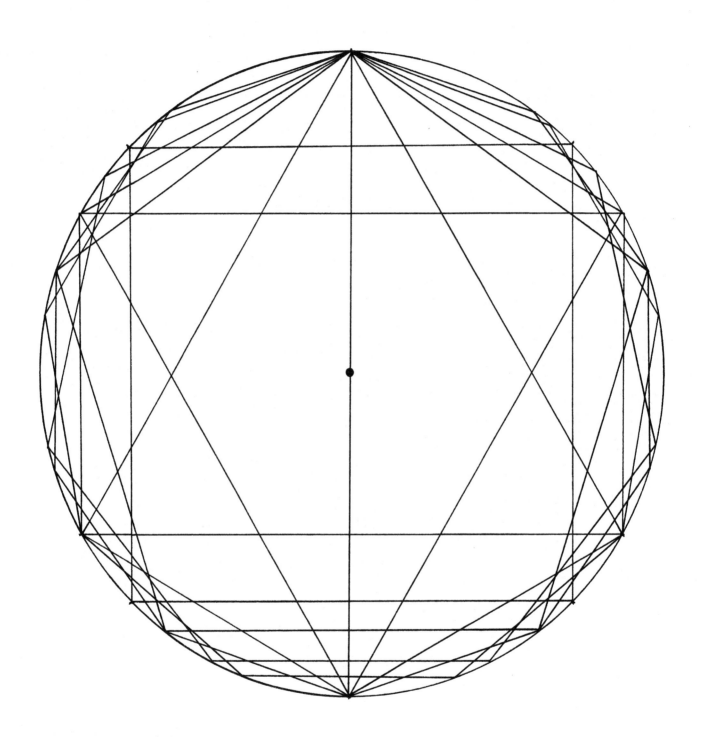

DRAWING SACRED GEOMETRY MANDALAS

THE DRAWINGS IN THIS CHAPTER present the basic form vocabulary for all the sacred geometry mandalas in this book. Their sequence follows the traditional Pythagorean numbering system one through ten. The geometric forms for each number, respectively, are: circle, semicircle, triangle, square, pentagon, hexagon, heptagon, octagon, nonagon, and decagon. Pythagoras saw in this progression of forms the natural process of things coming into being. Drawing these geometric figures in the order given here will help you grasp the way each form builds on its predecessor, so you can get a better sense of the Pythagorean ideas. I also include geometric forms for eleven (hendecagon), twelve (dodecagon), and thirteen (tridecagon).

Opposite: This mandala illustrates all of the geometric
forms associated with the Pythagorean numbers 1 through 10:
circle, semicircle, triangle, square, pentagon, hexagon,
heptagon, octagon, nonagon, and decagon.

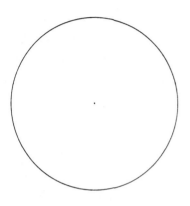

CIRCLE (PYTHAGOREAN ONE)

To draw a circle, place the point of a compass near the center of a piece of paper. Move the pencil end of the compass in a circle around the center while keeping the point in contact with the center point of the paper.

SEMICIRCLE (PYTHAGOREAN TWO)

To draw a semicircle, first draw a circle as described above. Establish a line AB perpendicular to the bottom of your paper, passing through the center of the circle. This line bisects the circle into two equal halves.

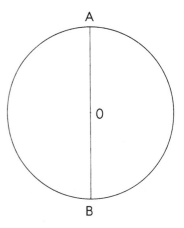

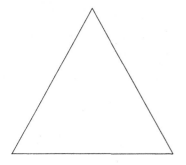

TRIANGLE (PYTHAGOREAN THREE)

To create a triangle, draw a circle with center point O bisected by line AB. With your compass on the same setting you used to draw the circle, place the point at B and draw an arc intersecting the original circle in two places, points C and D (see Triangle 1). Then connect points A, D, and C with straight lines.

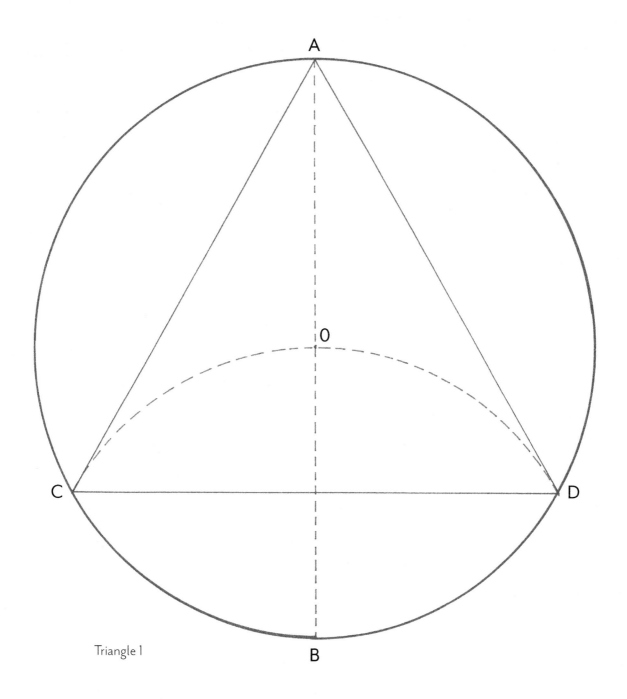

Triangle 1

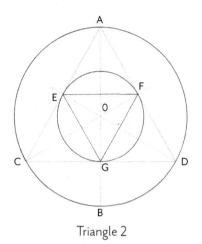

Triangle 2

Elaborating on the Triangle

Place the point of the compass on the center point O and adjust the radius to touch the sides of the triangle described above. Draw a circle inside the triangle (see Triangle 2). Bisect the triangle by drawing a line from point C through O to point F on the opposite side of the triangle, creating line CF. Following the same procedure, draw line D through O to establish E, and line DE. Connect points E, F, and G to create a new triangle.

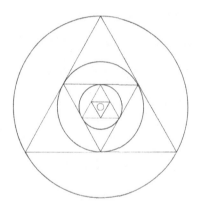

Triangle 3

Triangle and Circle Progression

Continue the procedure described for Triangle 2 to create smaller and smaller circles and triangles inside the original circle. Tip: use a circle template to draw the small inner circles, as shown in Triangle 3.

Mandorla

Draw a circle with the center point O bisected by line AB. Adjust your compass one inch wider. Set the compass point at A and scribe arcs as shown in Triangle 4. Then set the point of your compass at B and scribe arcs that intersect the two arcs just drawn. Draw a line through these intersection points and center point O, establishing points C and D. Now set your compass to be *one inch more* than approximately *half the distance* between points C and O. With the compass point at C draw two arcs as shown. Place the compass point at D and scribe two arcs. Now place the compass point at O and draw arcs that intersect all four of the previously drawn arcs.

Draw a line, using the intersections of the arcs, to divide line CO in half at point E. Do the same to find the center of line DO at point F. Adjust the compass back to the radius of the original circle. Place the point of the compass at E and draw a circle. Place the point of the compass at F and draw a circle. You have created a *mandorla,* or *vesica piscis* (see Triangle 5).

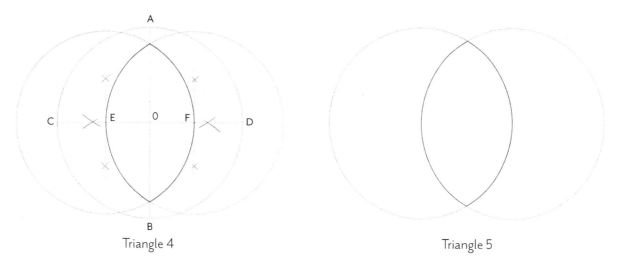

Triangle 4

Triangle 5

SQUARE (PYTHAGOREAN FOUR)

To create a square, draw a circle with the center point O bisected by line AB. Set the compass point at A and scribe arcs outside the circle as shown in Square 1. Place the compass point at B and repeat the procedure. Set the compass one inch larger and then place the point of the compass at A and scribe arcs inside the circle, in the left and right halves of the circle. Move the compass point to B and repeat the procedure.

Draw a line through the intersection points of the arcs and O, the center of the circle, creating line CD. Then draw lines connecting the intersection points of the arcs *outside* the circle, through center point O, as shown in Square 2. Now connect the points where the lines intersect the circle to create a square resting on its side, or a square dancing on its point (see Square 3). You may also use the intersection points of the arcs outside the circle to delineate a square *outside* the circle whose sides touch the circle.

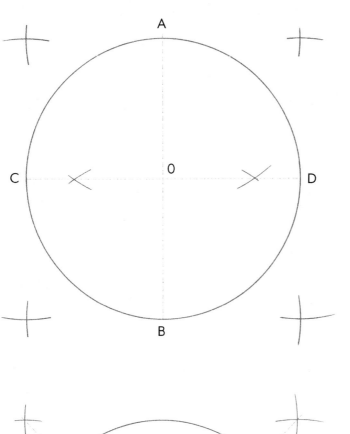

Square 1

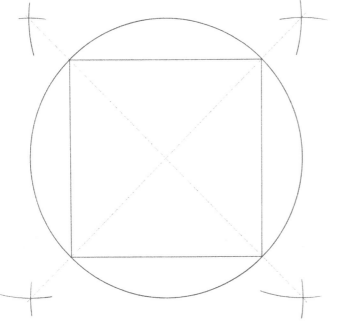

Square 2

Still and Dancing Squares Mandala

Working on the figure established in Square 3, you can add additional lines as shown in Square 4. See how smaller and smaller squares alternate in an infinite regression toward zero, at the center of the circle.

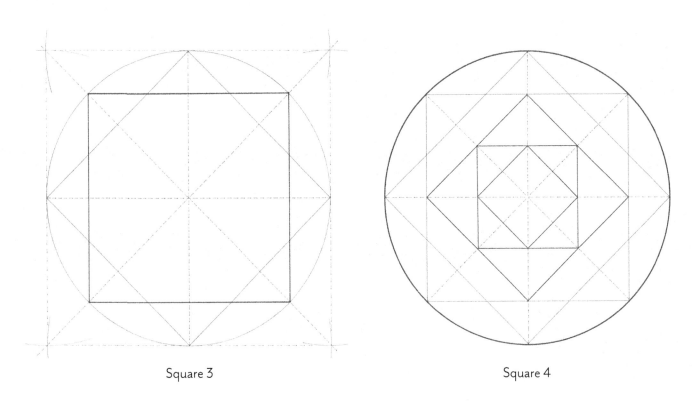

Square 3

Square 4

Scalloped Circles Mandala

This mandala is a variation on Square 4 incorporating circles. The smaller circles appear to be distorted, or scalloped, in an optical illusion created by the strong form of the squares and their points, which intersect the circles. This design is capable of an infinite regression to smaller and smaller iterations, even to the point of apparent nothingness, or zero.

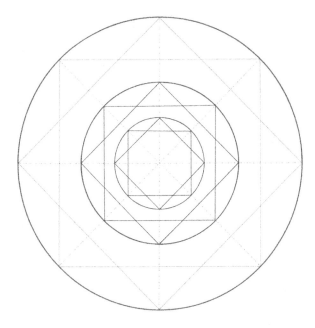

Square 5

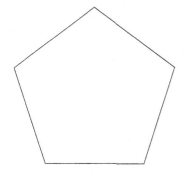

PENTAGON (PYTHAGOREAN FIVE)

Draw a circle with center point O intersected by line AB. Using a protractor, measure and draw line CD at right angles (90 degrees) from line AB. Place your compass point at C and draw an arc intersecting the circle at points E and G (see Pentagon 1). Place the point of your compass at D and repeat this procedure to establish points F and H. Draw a line from E to G, intersecting line CO at center I. Draw a line from F to H, intersecting line OD at center J.

Adjust your compass to draw a circle centered at point I, touching the outer circle and its center point O (see Pentagon 2). Place the point of your compass at J and repeat to create a second circle of the same size on the opposite side of the circle.

Now place your compass point at B and adjust your compass to draw an arc that just touches the two smaller circles (see Pentagon 3). It will intersect your original circle at points K and L. Connect points K and L with a straight line. Line KL is the base of your pentagon.

Set your compass to the length of line KL. Place the point of your compass on L and scribe an arc that will intersect the original circle at points K and M (see Pentagon 4). Then place your compass point at point K and draw an arc that intersects the circle at points N and L. Now connect points A, M, L, K, N, and A with straight lines to create your pentagon (see Pentagon 5).[1]

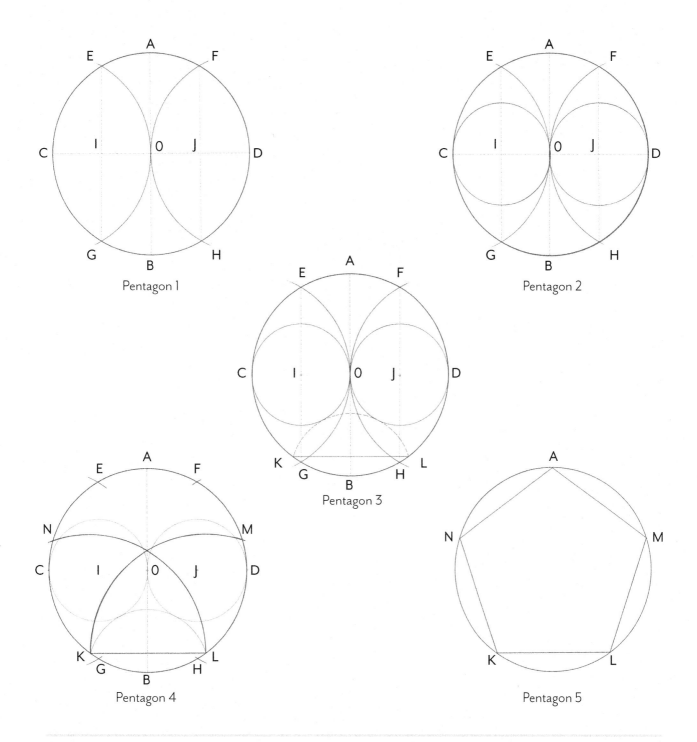

Pentagon 1

Pentagon 2

Pentagon 3

Pentagon 4

Pentagon 5

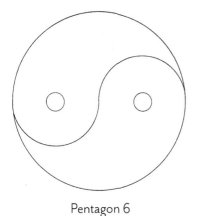

Pentagon 6

Yin Yang Mandala

You will notice that Pentagon 2 creates the structure for the familiar yin yang symbol (see Pentagon 6), signifying a balancing of opposites.

Five-Pointed Star Mandala

After completing a pentagon drawing (Pentagon 5), draw a straight line starting from point A at the top of the circle, moving clockwise, skipping the next point M, and connecting to point L. Continuing clockwise, put your pencil on point M, skip point L, and connect a line to point K. Continue in this manner, connecting *every other* point of the pentagon with straight lines. When all points are connected, you will have a five-pointed star (see Pentagon 7). The star has been created with one continuous line, forming a symbolic protection. You will notice that there is a pentagon inside the star. You can draw more pentagons and stars as demonstrated in Pentagon 8.

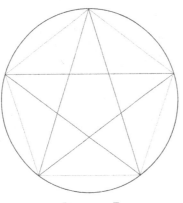

Pentagon 7

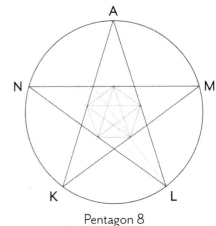

Pentagon 8

Infinite Pentagons Mandala

After constructing the pentagon shown in Pentagon 5, draw lines to connect each point of the pentagon with the midpoint of its opposite side (see Pentagon 9). Connecting the midpoints with lines produces a smaller upside-down pentagon. Continue in this way to produce smaller and smaller pentagons, alternately right-side up and upside down.

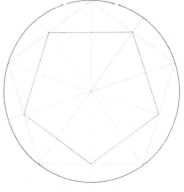

Pentagon 9

Nautilus Shell Mandala

The Infinite Pentagons Mandala can be colored as shown in Pentagon 10 to highlight the graceful curve of a regression toward the ultimate center point, or zero, creating a spiral, or nautilus shell, effect.

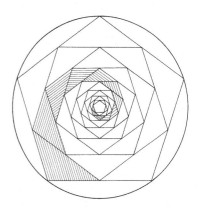

Pentagon 10

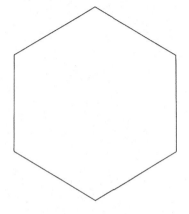

HEXAGON (PYTHAGOREAN SIX)

Draw a circle with center point O bisected by line AB. Place the point of the compass on point A and scribe an arc intersecting the circle at points C and D, as shown in Hexagon 1. Place the compass point at C and draw an arc, intersecting the circle at points A and E. Repeat these steps to create a *flower* with six petals (see Hexagon 2). The points of the petals mark six points along the circle. Moving clockwise from A, draw a straight line to points D, F, B, E, C, and back to A to form a hexagon balancing on its point.

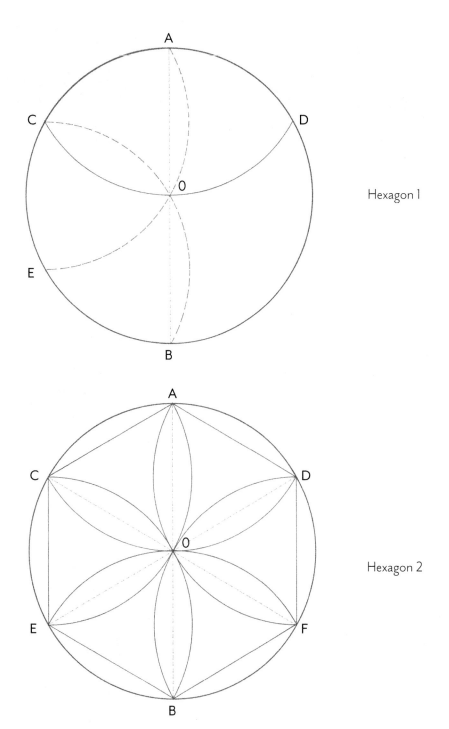

Hexagon 1

Hexagon 2

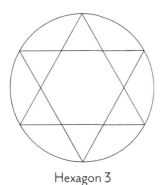

Hexagon 3

Star of David or Solomon's Seal Mandala

Using the points on Hexagon 2 as your guide, you may construct two intersecting triangles to form this ancient symbol (see Hexagon 3). Draw a straight line starting from point A at the top of the circle and, moving clockwise, skipping the next point D, and connecting to point F. Then draw a line from F to E and from E back to A. Continuing clockwise, put your pencil on point D, skip point F, and connect a line to point B. Then draw a line from B to C and back to D.

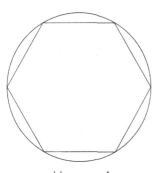

Hexagon 4

Hexagon on a Base

To draw a hexagon resting on one of its flat sides (see Hexagon 4), draw a line AB (see Hexagon 5) and set your compass to the length of that line. Place your compass point at A and draw a circle. Keeping your compass adjustment the same, place the compass point on B and draw another circle. Place the point of your compass on the intersection of the two circles above the line (C) and draw a circle. Again keeping your compass on the same setting, place the compass point at D and draw an arc that intersects the circle at F. Move the compass point to E and draw an arc that intersects the circle at G. Connect points B, A, D, F, G, E, and B to complete the hexagon (see Hexagon 6).

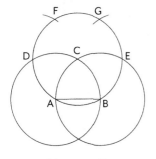

Hexagon 5

Hexagon 6

Mandala of Six Circles

Draw a circle and establish perpendicular line AB. Using your protractor, measure and mark six 60-degree angles along the circle (see Hexagon 2). Align a straightedge and draw lines DE and FC through opposite angle marks and passing through center O. Adjust your compass to about half the width desired for the center area of the mandala. Place the compass point at center O and scribe a circle. Reset your compass to draw a circle with a radius one inch *smaller* than your *original* circle. Place the compass point at the intersection of line OA and the smaller circle and draw a circle. Now move the compass point to the intersection of line OD and the smaller circle and draw a circle. Continue until six circles have been drawn.

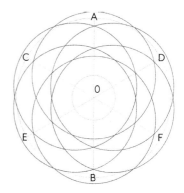

Hexagon 7

Mandala with Interlacing Circles

Continue working on the mandala drawing in Hexagon 7 described above. Set your compass to draw a circle with a radius 1/2 inch smaller than that used to scribe the six circles in Hexagon 7. Draw circles from each intersection, as above, except that these circles have a smaller radius. This produces the appearance of ribbon or interlacing. Create over and under intersections as shown in Hexagon 8. Place the compass point on center O and adjust to draw a circle that will appear to go behind interlacing ribbon lines, as shown. Use a circle template to draw the smallest inner circles.

Hexagon 8

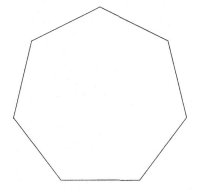

HEPTAGON (PYTHAGOREAN SEVEN)

Draw a circle with center O inside a square (refer to Square 3 on page 52). Set your compass to the length of the line between points E and F (see Heptagon 1). Place your compass on E and draw an arc that intersects line AB. Now place your compass at point F and swing an arc that intersects your previous arc on line AB. This intersection is point J. Note that you have also created intersections at points K and L on your circle. Adjust your compass to the distance between points A and K. Moving counter-clockwise around the circle, place the point of your compass on point K and swing an arc intersecting the circle. Move the point of your compass to this new intersection point, and scribe the next arc, intersecting the circle. Continue in this manner around the circle at point Q. At point L, check your accuracy. Adjust your compass as necessary to have all segments of the circle the same, and end neatly at point L. Connect points A, L, M, N, P, Q, K, and ending at A (see Heptagon 2).

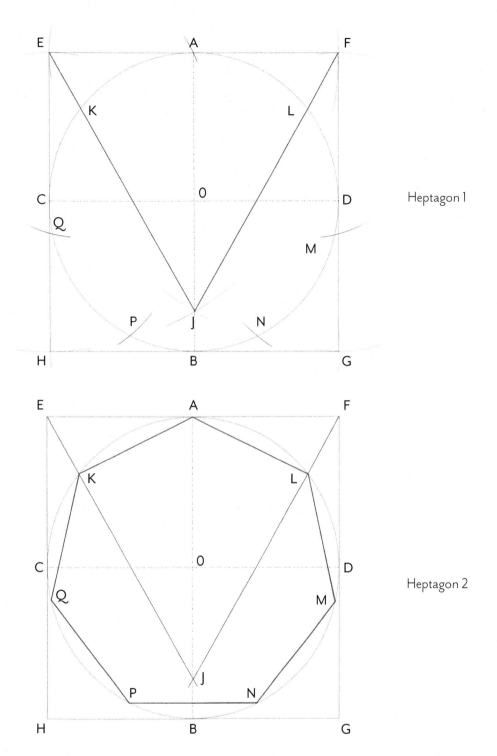

Heptagon 1

Heptagon 2

Heptagon Star Mandala One

Using your heptagon figure as a guide, connect *every other* point with straight lines (see Heptagon 3).

Heptagon Star Mandala Two

Using your heptagon figure as a guide, connect every *third* point, skipping *two* points in between each connecting point (see Heptagon 4). One continuous line forms this star, and, because of this, in the ancient world it was thought to provide a spiritual protection.

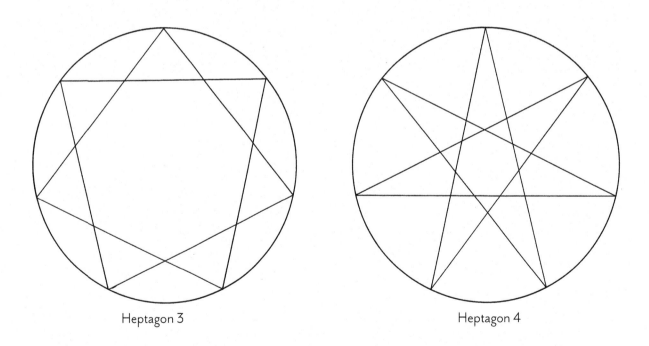

Heptagon 3   Heptagon 4

Seven-Petaled Flower Mandala

Using your heptagon figure (Heptagon 2) as a guide, set your compass to the distance between point A and point L on the circle. Place the compass point on point A and scribe an arc intersecting the circle at points C and D. Moving clockwise, place the point of your compass on point D and scribe an arc. Continue in this way until you have drawn an arc from each of the seven points of the heptagon along the circle. Now adjust your compass to a 1/4 to 1/2 inch wider setting. Place the point of the compass at point A and swing an arc. Continue from point to point scribing arcs as before. Now adjust your compass to approximately one inch smaller than the original radius setting of the circle. Place the point of the compass at point A and swing an arc. Continue in this manner as before. Erase the arc where it intersects a petal, as shown in Heptagon 5.

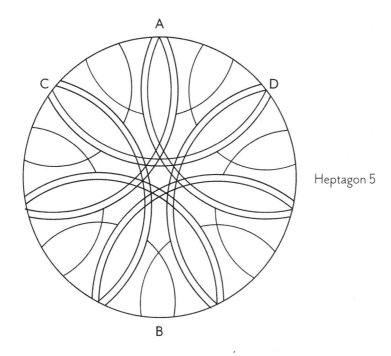

Heptagon 5

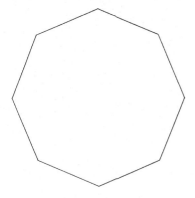

OCTAGON (PYTHAGOREAN EIGHT)

Draw a circle with center O intersected by perpendicular line AB (see Octagon 1). Using a protractor, measure and mark angles at 90 degrees and 270 degrees. Draw a line through center O connecting these points and intersecting the circle at points C and D. Keeping your compass set on the radius of your original circle, place the compass point at A and draw two arcs above and outside the circle as shown. Next, place the compass point at B and repeat, drawing arcs below and outside the circle. Move the compass to points C and then D, scribing arcs that intersect the previously drawn arcs. Draw lines through O connecting opposite intersecting arcs outside the circle. These lines intersect the circle at four points: E, F, G, and H. Connect these four points and points A, E, D, F, B, G, C, H, and A to form your octagon.

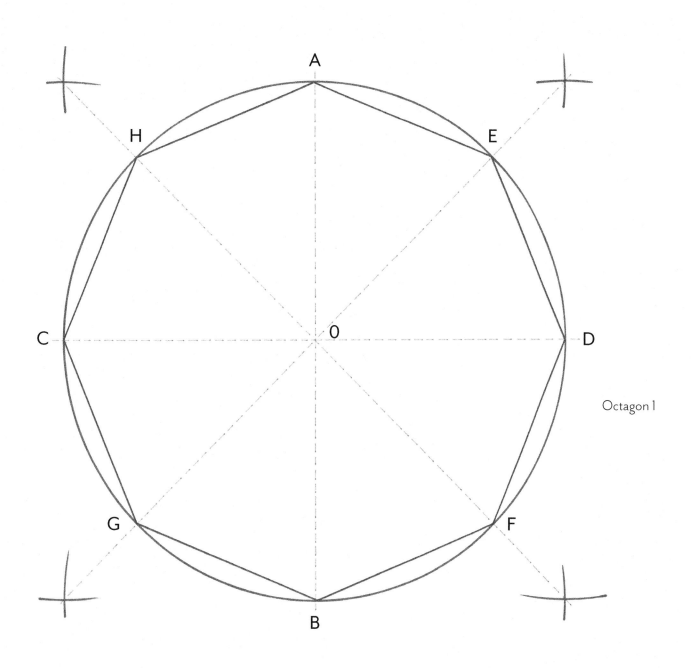

Octagon 1

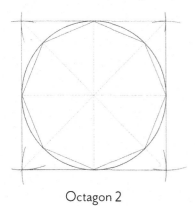

Octagon 2

Octagon Inside a Square

Continuing on from Octagon 1, connect the arc intersection points with straight lines to establish a square *outside* the octagon (see Octagon 2).

Octagon on a Base

Draw a circle inside a square, following the steps outlined for Octagon 1. Then set your compass to the distance between O and E (see Octagon 3), place the compass point on O, and draw a circle enclosing the square. Extend lines AB and CD to intersect the outside circle, creating points A^1, B^1, C^1, and D^1. Starting at A^1, connect points D^1, B^1, C^1, and back to A^1 to create a square resting on its tip (see Octagon 4). Now draw lines as shown in Octagon 5 to complete the octagon on a base.

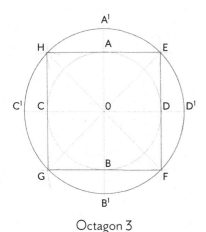

Octagon 3

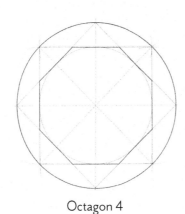

Octagon 4

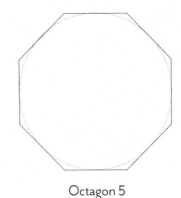

Octagon 5

Octagon Star Mandala One

Using your octagon as a guideline, draw lines to connect *every other* point of your octagon (see Octagon 6).

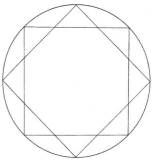

Octagon 6

Octagon Star Mandala Two

Using your octagon as a guideline, draw lines to connect every *third* point, skipping *two* points in between each connecting point (see Octagon 7). This star is formed by a continuous line, which is unusual for a figure with an even number of points. This may, in part, explain the traditional importance given to the octagon.

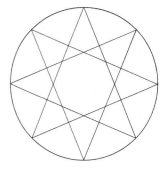

Octagon 7

Crystal Mandala

Using your octagon as a guideline, begin at point A and draw lines to connect *every other* point, as in Octagon 6. Begin again at point A and draw lines to connect every *third* point, skipping *two* points in between connecting points, as shown in Octagon 7. Using Octagon 8 as a guide, add and erase lines to create the Crystal Mandala.

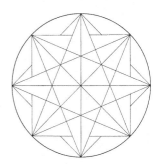

Octagon 8

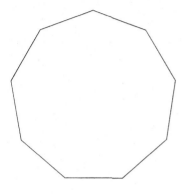

NONAGON, OR ENNEAGON (PYTHAGOREAN NINE)

Draw a circle with center point O divided by lines AB and CD (see Nonagon 1). Adjust your compass to the length between point A and point C. With your compass point at A draw arc CD. The arc intersects line AB at point E. Adjust your compass to *1/2 inch more than half* the distance between E and B. With the point at E, draw two arcs as shown. Place your compass point on B and draw two arcs that intersect the two arcs just drawn. The line between these two points of intersection will bisect line EB and establish point F.

Adjust your compass to the distance between points E and F. Place your compass on F and draw a circle that fits precisely between the arc CD and the original circle. From point A draw lines on either side of the small circle (see Nonagon 2). These lines intersect the outside circle to establish points G and H. The line between G and H is one side of your nonagon. Set your compass for the distance between G and H, and moving your compass from point to point around the circle, mark nine points. Connect the nine points to create a nonagon. You will probably find that you do not hit the final mark with precision. Adjust your compass slightly until you can mark off nine equal segments.

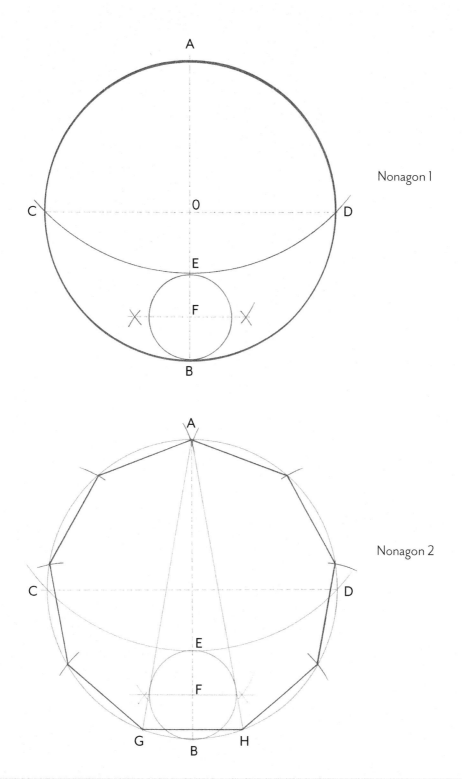

Nonagon 1

Nonagon 2

Nonagon Star Mandala One

Using your nonagon figure as your guide, connect *every other* point with straight lines (see Nonagon 3).

Nonagon Star Mandala Two

Using your nonagon figure as a starting point, connect every *third* point, skipping *two* points between each connection point. You will notice that you create three overlapping equilateral triangles (all sides equal) in this mandala (see Nonagon 4).

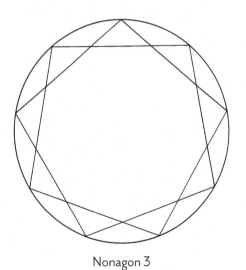

Nonagon 3

Nonagon 4

Nonagon Star Mandala Three

Once again using your nonagon figure as a guide, connect the points, skipping *three* points between connecting points (see Nonagon 5). This star is formed by a simple continuous line, "covering all sections of the figure in the accepted tradition of continuous enclosures representing spiritual protection."[2]

Nonagon Crystal Mandala

Follow the directions for creating Nonagon Star One (Nonagon 3). Overlay the design for Nonagon Star Mandala Two (Nonagon 4) and then overlay the design for Nonagon Star Mandala Three (Nonagon 5) to complete the Nonagon Crystal Mandala (see Nonagon 6).

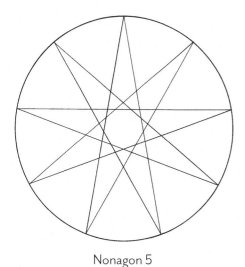

Nonagon 5

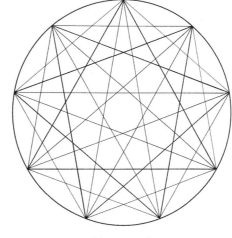

Nonagon 6

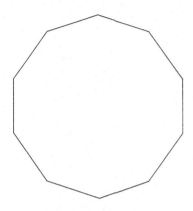

DECAGON (PYTHAGOREAN TEN)

To create a decagon, first draw a pentagon as directed in Pentagon 3 (see page 54). Then draw a line from each point through the center point O to intersect the point on the opposite side of the circle (see Decagon 1). Now simply connect the points along the circle to create a decagon.

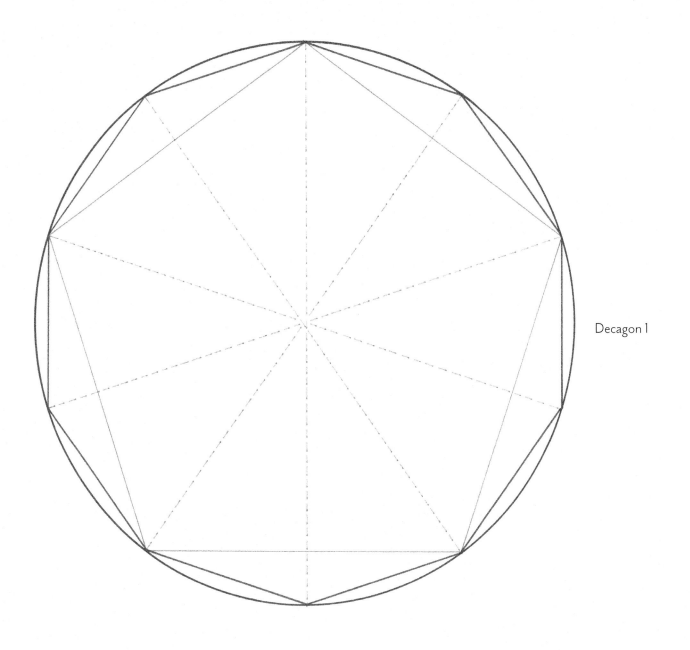

Decagon 1

Decagon Star Mandala One

Using your completed decagon as a starting point, connect *every other* point with straight lines (see Decagon 2).

Decagon Star Mandala Two

Beginning with your decagon, connect every *third* point with lines, skipping *two* points between connections (see Decagon 3).

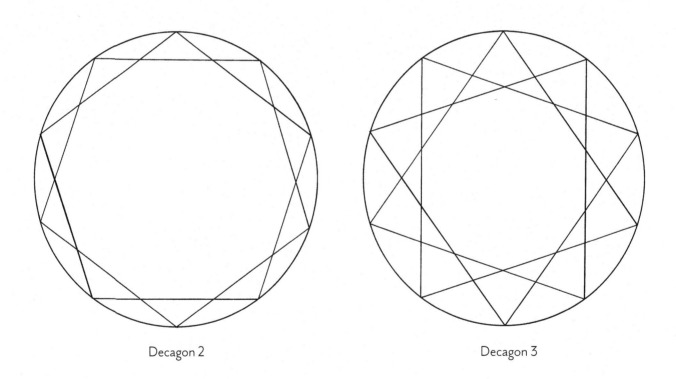

Decagon 2   Decagon 3

Decagon Star Mandala Three

Connecting the ten points of your decagon, connect every *fourth* point, skipping *three* points between connections. Your completed mandala consists of five overlapping five-pointed stars (see Decagon 4).

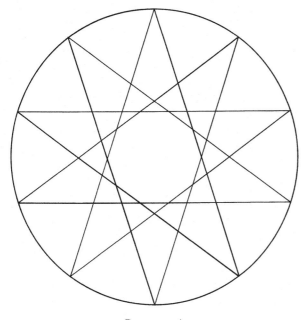

Decagon 4

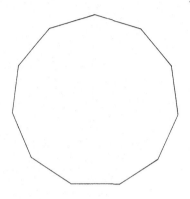

HENDECAGON, OR ELEVEN-SIDED MANDALA

Draw a circle with center point O intersected by perpendicular line AB. Use your protractor to measure and mark eleven angles of approximately 32.5 degrees (see Hendecagon 1). Draw lines between center O and the circle, using the protractor measurement marks as your guide. Connect the eleven intersection points on the circle with straight lines.

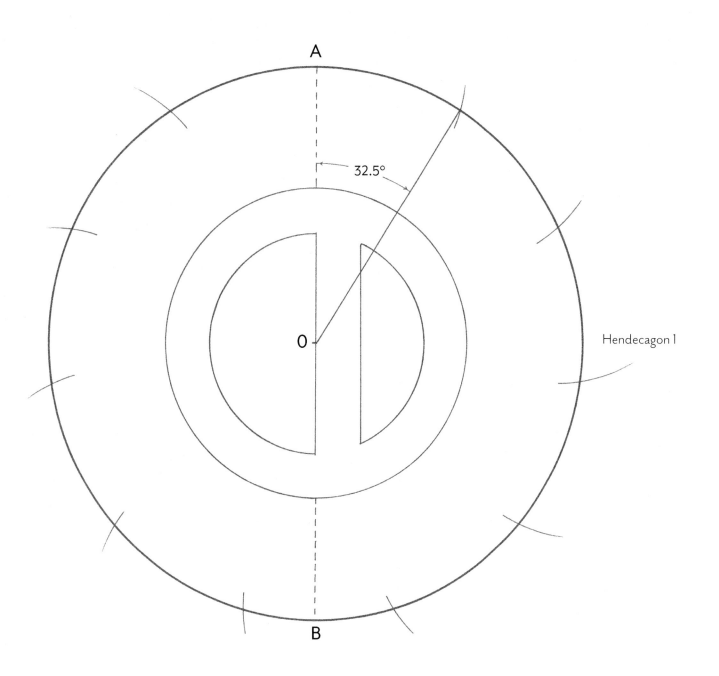

A

32.5°

0

B

Hendecagon 1

Hendecagon Star Mandala One

Beginning at point A of your hendecagon, connect *every other* point (see Hendecagon 2).

Hendecagon Star Mandala Two

Connect every *third* point of your hendecagon, skipping *two* points between each connecting point (see Hendecagon 3). This star is created with one continuous line connecting all points in order.

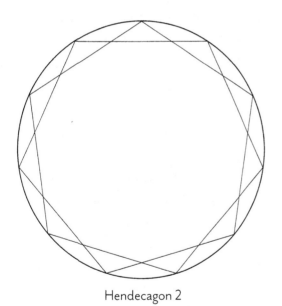

Hendecagon 2

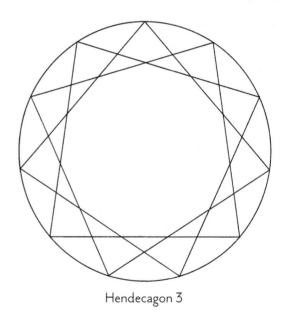

Hendecagon 3

Hendecagon Star Mandala Three

Connect the points of your hendecagon skipping *three* points between connections (see Hendecagon 4).

Hendecagon Star Mandala Four

Connect the points of your hendecagon, skipping *four* points between connections (see Hendecagon 5). One continuous line creates this complex mandala star.

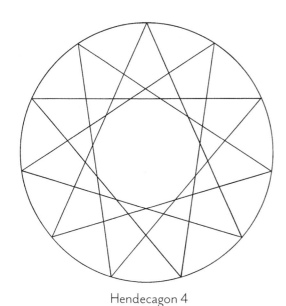

Hendecagon 4

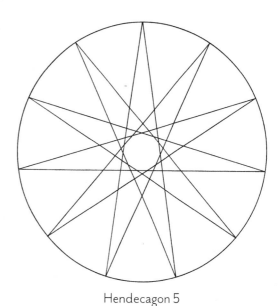

Hendecagon 5

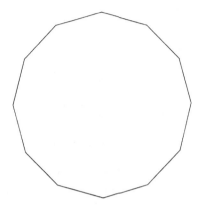

DODECAGON, OR TWELVE-SIDED MANDALA

Draw a hexagram as shown in Hexagon 2 (see page 59). Then connect points to create a figure, as shown in Hexagon 3 (see page 60). Using the intersection points of the two overlapping triangles as a guide, draw lines from side to side of the circle through the center of the circle (see Dodecagon 1). Keeping your compass on the same adjustment as for the radius of the original circle, place the point on the circle where one of the dotted lines intersects it. Draw arcs from here and other "empty" points to double the number of petals to twelve (see Dodecagon 2). Connect tips of petals to create the twelve-sided dodecagon.

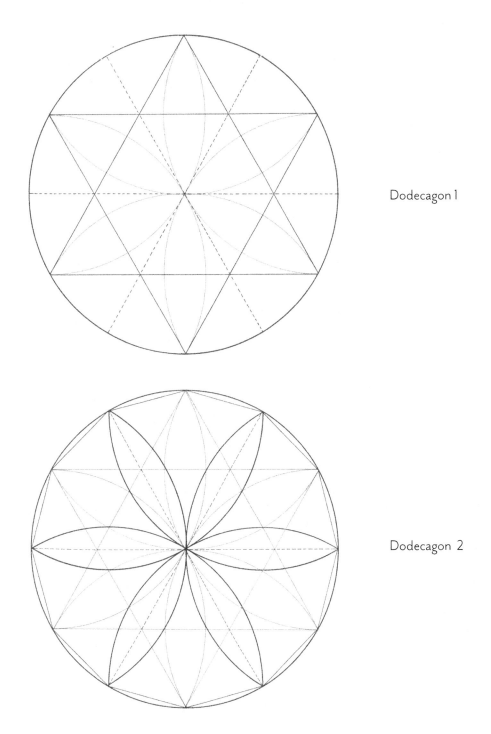

Dodecagon 1

Dodecagon 2

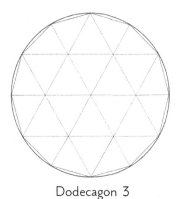

Dodecagon 3

Dodecagon Grid Mandala

With your dodecagon drawn, connect points as shown in Dodecagon 3 to create precisely divided triangular spaces inside the figure.

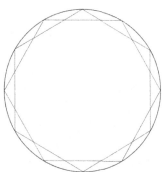
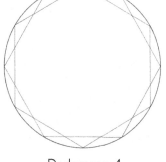

Dodecagon 4

Dodecagon Star Mandala One

With your dodecagon established, connect *every other* point to create this star mandala (see Dodecagon 4).

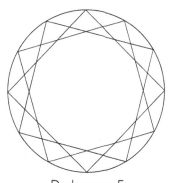

Dodecagon 5

Dodecagon Star Mandala Two

Using your dodecagon as a guide, connect every *third* point, skipping *two* points between connections (see Dodecagon 5).

Dodecagon Star Mandala Three

Begin with your dodecagon and connect every *fourth* point, skipping *three* points between connections (see Dodecagon 6).

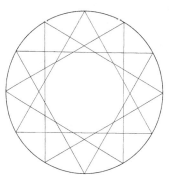

Dodecagon 6

Dodecagon Star Mandala Four

From a dodecagon figure, connect every *fifth* point, skipping *four* points between connections (see Dodecagon 7).

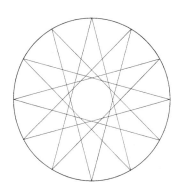

Dodecagon 7

Splendid Triangles Mandala

Beginning with the Dodecagon Star Mandala Three (Dodecagon 6), connect opposite points of the triangles (see Dodecagon 8). Use intersection points of triangles to establish additional lines between star points. Then draw a circle 1/2 inch *smaller* than the inner dodecagon created by overlapping triangles. Add a triangle and smaller circle as shown. Erase unnecessary guidelines in Dodecagon 8 to complete this mandala (see Dodecagon 9).

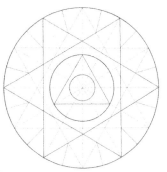

Dodecagon 8

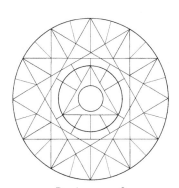

Dodecagon 9

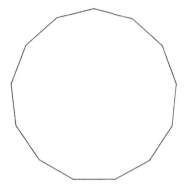

TRIDECAGON, OR THIRTEEN-SIDED MANDALA

Draw a circle with the center O, bisected by *horizontal* line AB (see Tridecagon 1). Using the same compass setting, place your compass point at A and draw a circle. Move the compass to B and draw a second circle. These two circles cross the original circle at points C, D, E, and F. Connecting these points you create a rectangle. A long side of the rectangle intersects line AB at point G. The distance between points G and E is the length of *each side* of the tridecagon. Set your compass to this distance.[3] Next, erect a line through the center of the center circle, perpendicular to line AB and bisecting the circle at point 1 (see Tridecagon 1)

Place the point of the compass at the top of the circle, point 1, and moving clockwise draw an arc intersecting the original circle. Continuing to move clockwise, place the point of the compass on this new intersection point and scribe an arc. Move the compass point to each new intersection point on the circle and swing an arc to find the next intersection point on the circle. As shown by the numbered points in Tridecagon 1, the circle will be intersected thirteen times. You will probably have to adjust your compass so that all segments of the circle are equal. To create the tridecagon, connect the intersection points on the circle with straight lines.

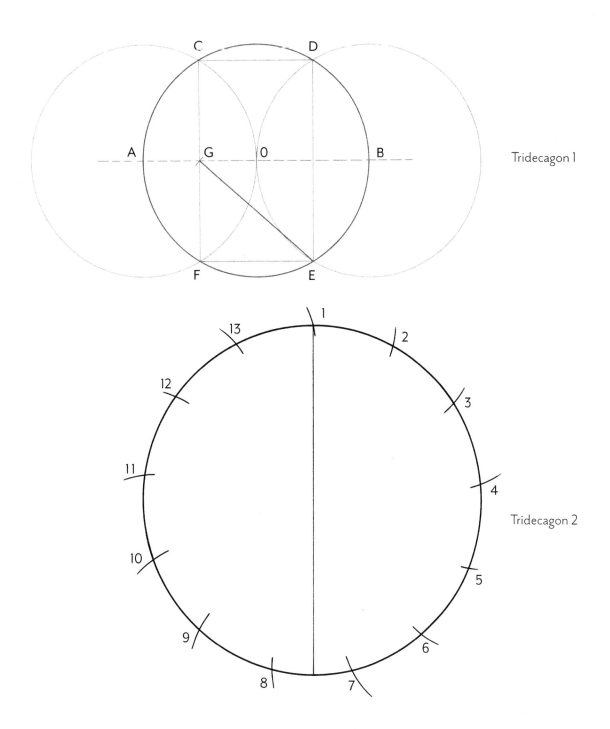

Tridecagon 1

Tridecagon 2

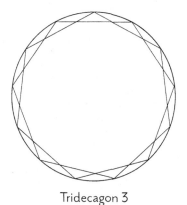

Tridecagon 3

Tridecagon Star Mandala One

Using the tridecagon figure you have drawn, connect *every other* point to create this mandala star (see Tridecagon 3).

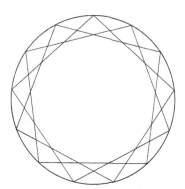

Tridecagon 4

Tridecagon Star Mandala Two

Working with a completed tridecagon figure, connect every *third* point, skipping *two* points between each connection (see Tridecagon 4).

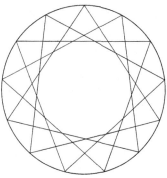

Tridecagon 5

Tridecagon Star Mandala Three

On a tridecagon figure, connect every *fourth* point, skipping *three* points between connections (see Tridecagon 5).

Tridecagon Star Mandala Four

Using a tridecagon as a starting point, connect every *fifth* point, skipping *four* points between connections (see Tridecagon 6).

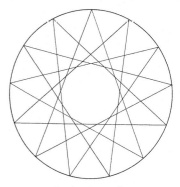

Tridecagon 6

Chartres Labyrinth Star

On the drawing of a tridecagon, connect every *sixth* point, skipping *five* points between connections (see Tridecagon 7). You will find that this complicated star can also be drawn with one continuous line, creating a figure thought to protect spiritual energy. This form underlies the structure of the Chartres Cathedral labyrinth (see text, pages 29–30).

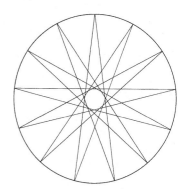

Tridecagon 7

Flower Petal Mandala

On the drawing of a tridecagon, set your compass to the distance between points 1 and 4. With the compass point at point 1, scribe an arc that connects points 4 and 11 (see Tridecagon 8). Keeping the same compass setting, place the compass point at point 2 and scribe another arc across the circle, connecting point 5 to point 12. Continue in this manner until you have completed thirteen petals.

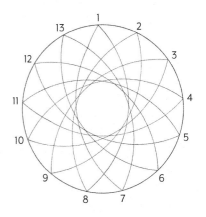

Tridecagon 8

Fantastic Flower Mandala

On the drawing of a tridecagon, with your compass set at the length of the radius of the circle, place your compass point at point 1 and scribe an arc that intersects the circle at two points (see Tridecagon 8). Move the point of your compass to point 2 and scribe an arc intersecting the circle at two points. Continue in this way around all thirteen points of the circle. Then adjust your compass to the distance between point 1 and point 2. Place the point of your compass at point 1 and scribe an arc. Move your compass point to point 2 and scribe an arc. Continue in this way around the thirteen points of the circle.

COLORING
SACRED GEOMETRY MANDALAS

COLOR ADDS a fascinating element to sacred geometry. With your color choices you can highlight areas of a geometric design so that they stand out and create the illusion of three-dimensional depth. Contrasting dark and light colors in your mandala makes lighter areas appear closer, while darker areas appear to sink into the background, giving a feeling of depth. Using colors that are similar, for example, all light pastels, emphasizes the design of the mandala's black lines. This tends to make the mandala appear like a unified whole. When you use several bright contrasting colors in your mandala, such as red, orange, green, blue, yellow, or purple, your mandala can appear to be many separate pieces, similar to a kaleidoscope.

Perhaps you will select colors intuitively, picking the one that attracts your attention first and letting that color guide the rest of your color choices. Or you might favor several colors that you like together and decide to use them throughout your mandala. Then again, you might want to choose colors by what they mean to you. For example, you might choose red because it symbolizes energy for you, and you want to include that quality in your mandala. Whatever you decide, just remember this: enjoy the process of coloring!

Reminiscent of a compass rose, this mandala demarcates four directions that serve as the basis for orientation in open space.

The hidden symmetry of a mandala grid underlies this whimsical mandala design of a face-to-face encounter among elfish folk. Pretend that they represent parts of you and color accordingly.

The Flower of Life affirms the visual rhythm established by repetition. Since the design can be enlarged infinitely—it has no designated end point—the Flower of Life communicates the ceaseless activity of growing things.

Note the geometric potential of circles to grow complex
interlacing designs that captivate the eye and excite the imagination
of what can be.

The Kabbalah Tree of Life illustrates the staged flow of God into his creation. The stages from one to ten are as follows: (1) Keter (Crown), (2) Hokhmah (Wisdom), (3) Binah (Intelligence), (4) Hesed (Mercy), (5) Din (Judgment) or Gevurah (Strength), (6) Tiferet (Beauty), (7) Netzah (Victory), (8) Hod (Splendor), (9) Yesod (Foundation), and (10) Malkhut (Kingdom).

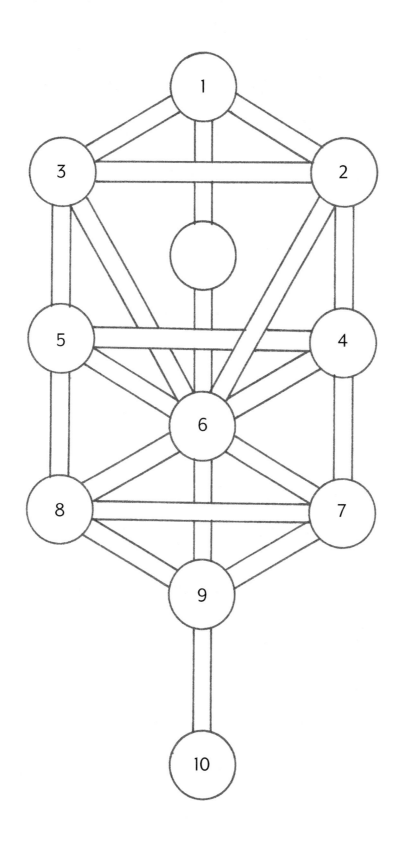

This mandala is a version of the South Asian Sri Yantra,
which represents masculine and feminine sacred energies
converging and interpenetrating.

Metatron's Cube is a representation of the elements of creation, according to ancient Greek tradition. It incorporates depictions of the Five Platonic Solids.

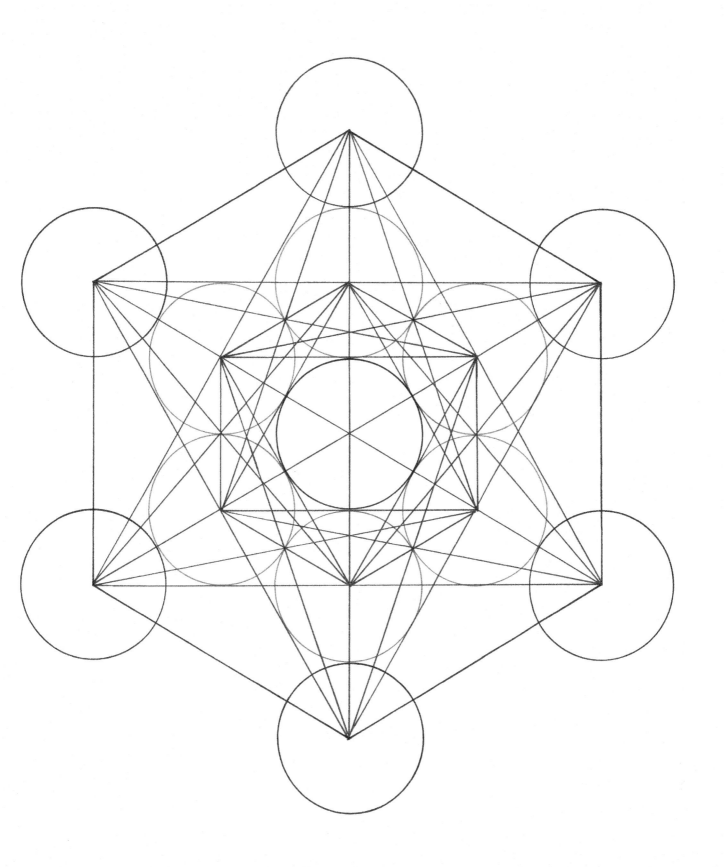

Pythagoras envisioned the numbers one through ten as geometric forms. This mandala is comprised of all of these geometric forms: circle (or point), semicircle (or line), triangle, square, pentagon, hexagon, heptagon, octagon, nonagon, and decagon.

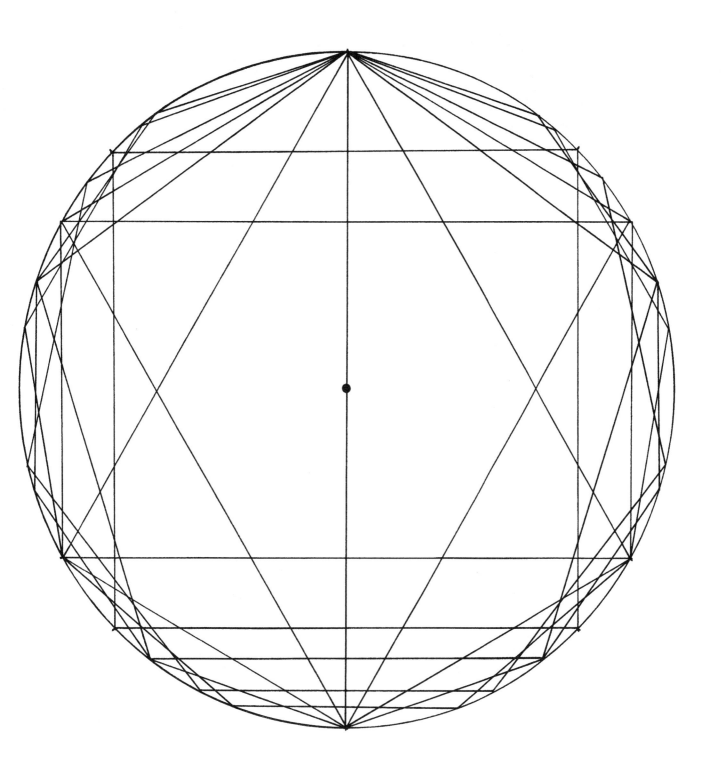

Circles and triangles alternate in this mandala, suggesting the process of growth.

The center almond shape is a mandorla. It symbolizes the convergence of two opposing elements into a third entity that incorporates qualities of both elements into a new and harmonious synthesis.

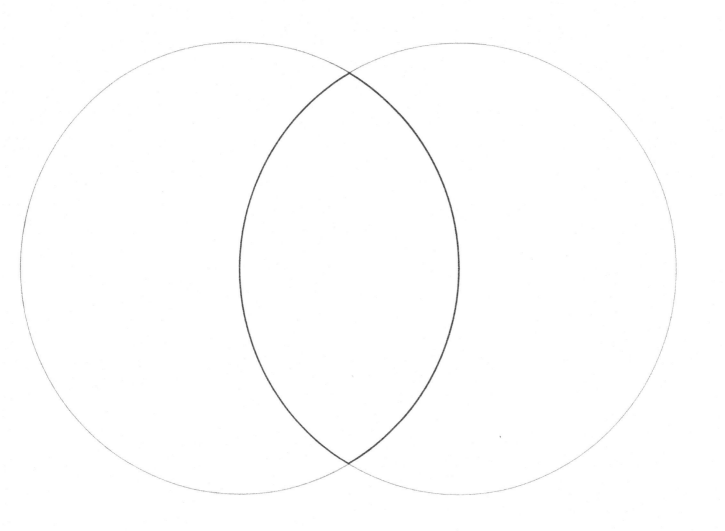

Your choice of color can give an impression of depth in this mandala.
To the human eye bright and light colors appear to come forward,
while dark colors seem to recede.

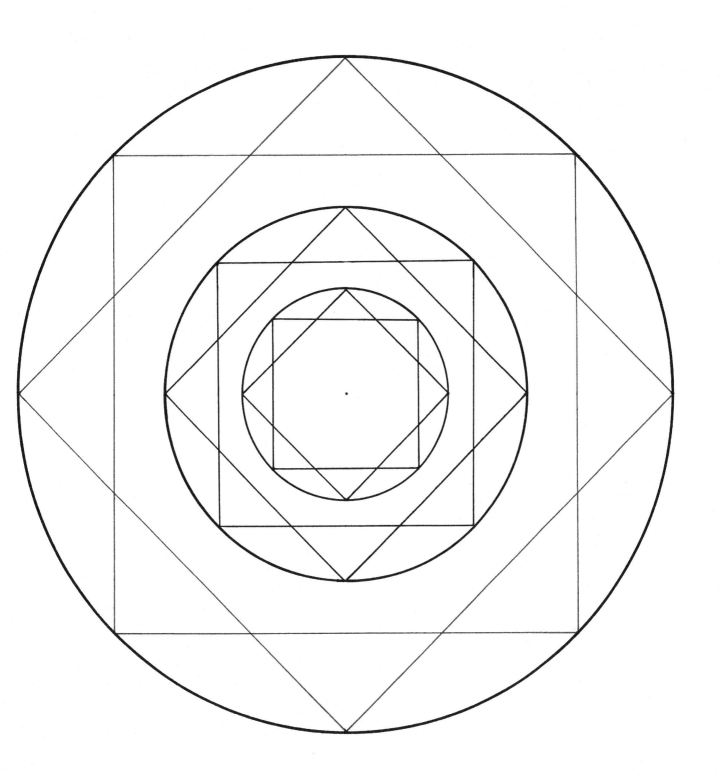

The yin yang is an ancient Chinese symbol of the dance of opposites, e.g., light and dark, masculine and feminine. In coloring this mandala, be open to the discovery that conflicts within and without can be reimagined as an archetypal dance that just *is*.

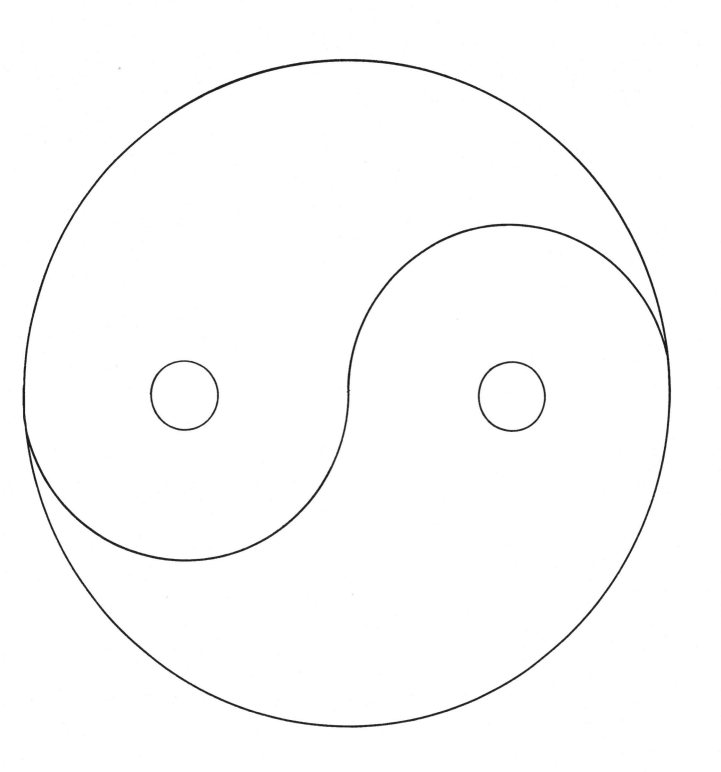

Play with this mandala of shrinking pentagons reminiscent
of the Fibonacci progression. Following the lead of the shaded
areas toward the center with your coloring may give you a sense
of the vanishing point of zero.

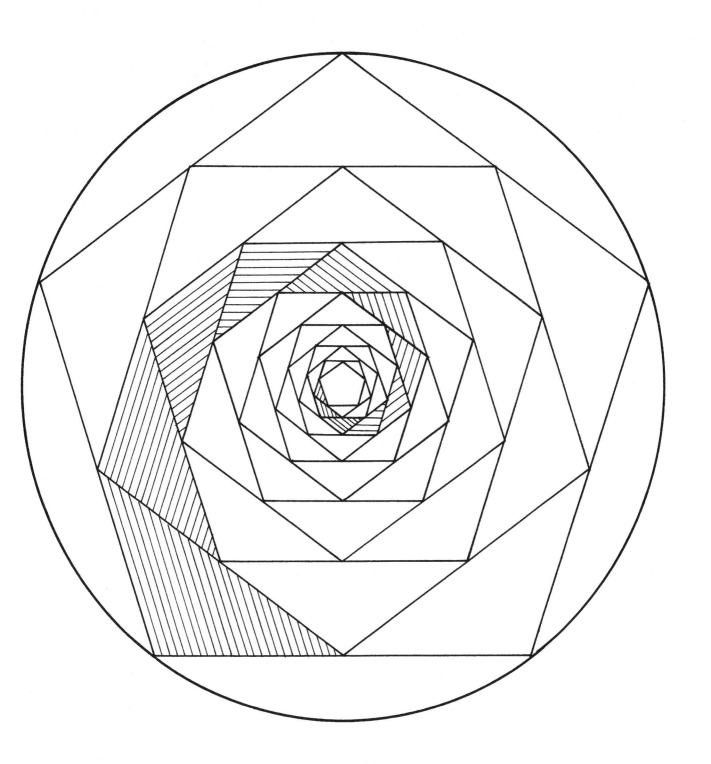

In this mandala seven circling pathways intertwine like the orbits of planets around a star. Perhaps the meaning of the colors you choose will reveal your inner constellations.

Here we see a mandala star design consisting of a single line connecting all seven points. In some traditions it is thought to offer protection from negative influences.

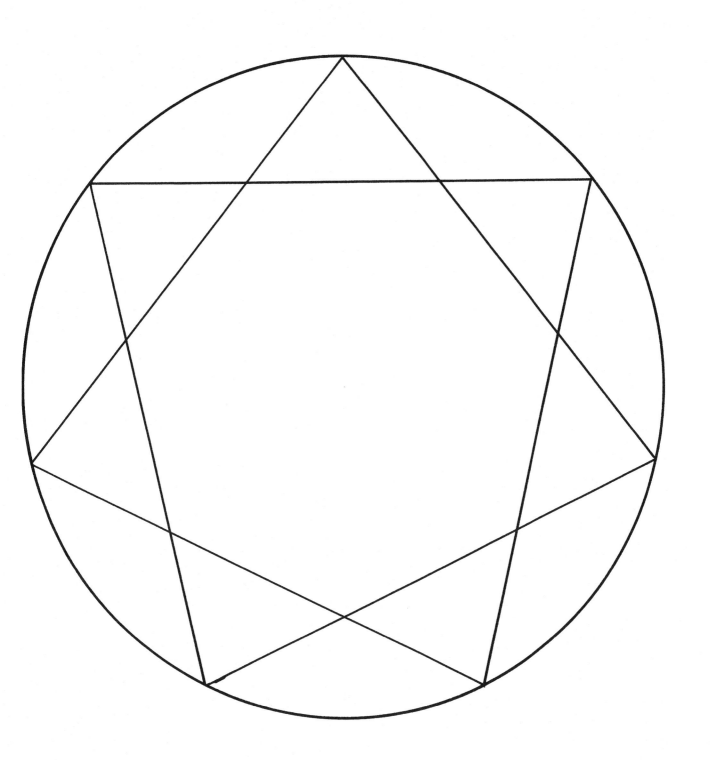

Based on the sacred number seven, this lively mandala design invites
exploration of over-and-under interlacements using colors and shading.

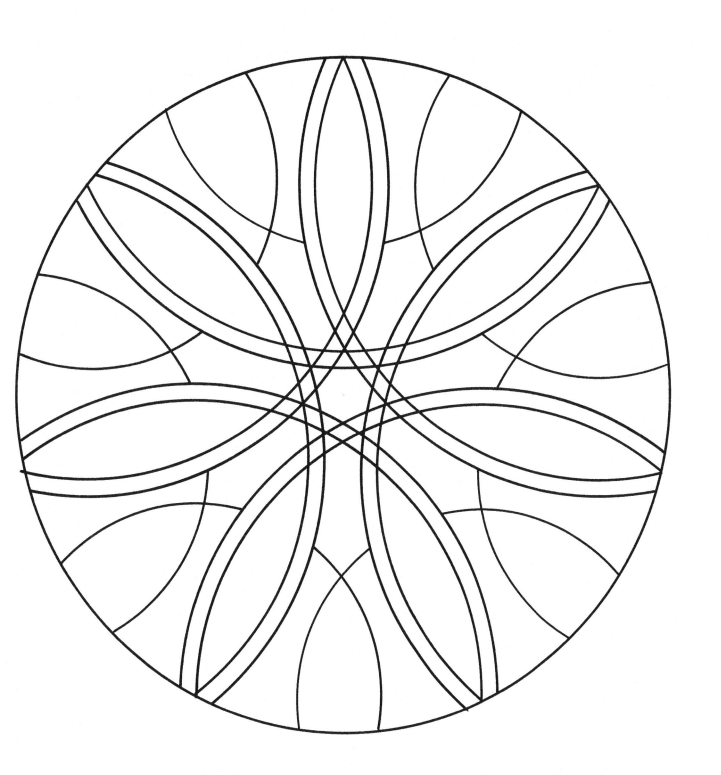

An eight-pointed star with an octagon at the center is an emphatic statement of the strength and balance of the number eight in Greek philosophy.

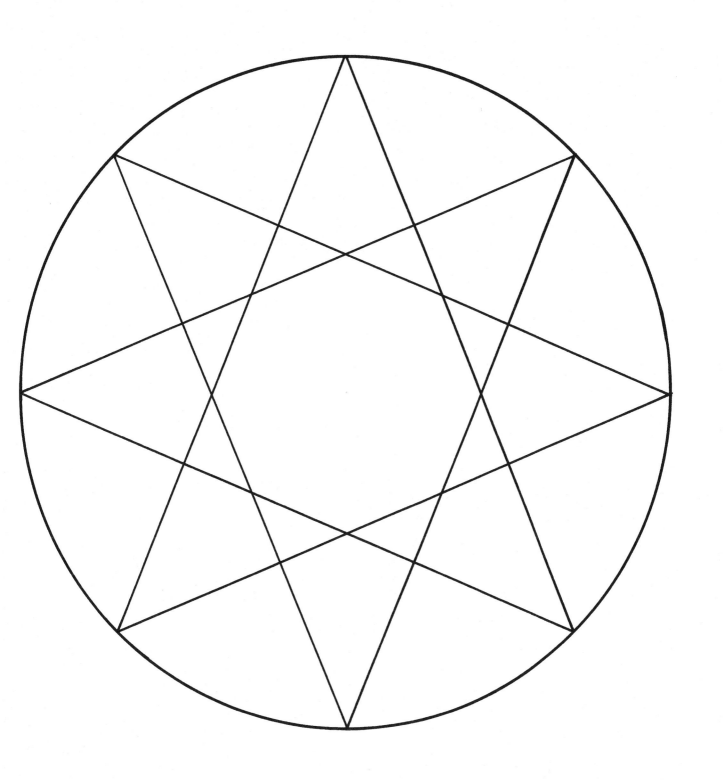

When star mandalas are overlaid, an octagon becomes a crystal.
Can you see the numerous triangles, squares, and five-pointed stars
competing for your attention?

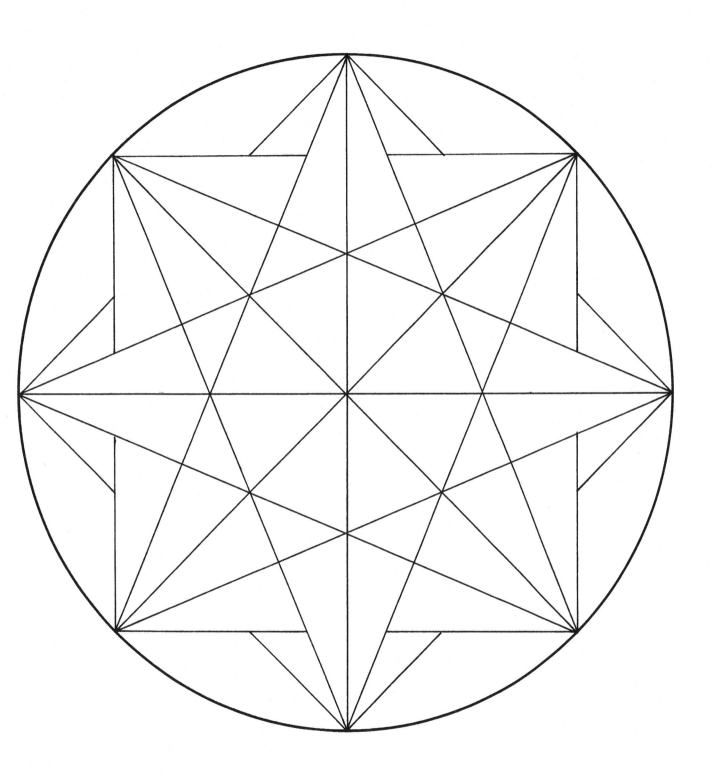

A continuous line interlaces to form this nine-pointed star, revered in ancient times as a protection from bad luck.

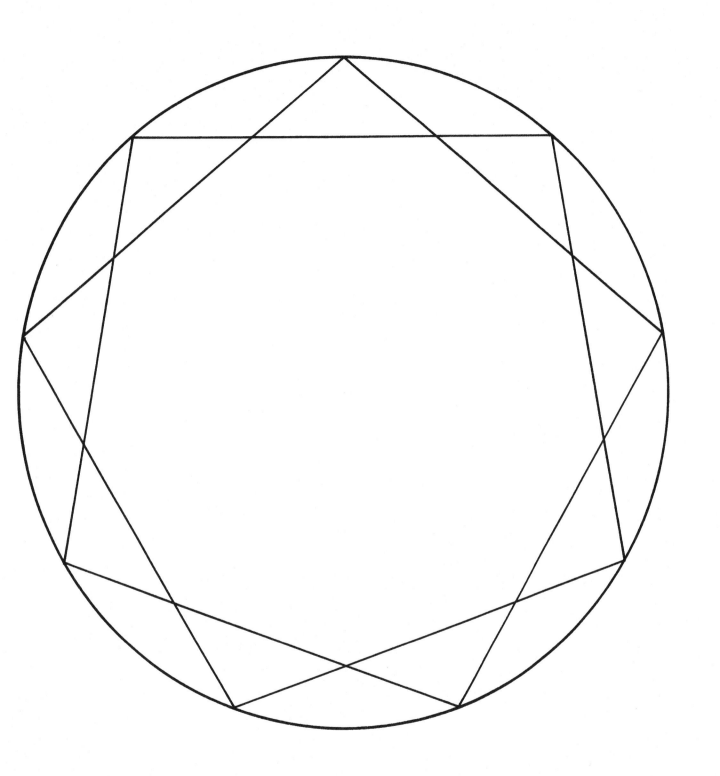

Three separate triangles form this nine-pointed star. The convergence of threes in this design makes it significant in the iconography of religions honoring trinitarian gods or goddesses.

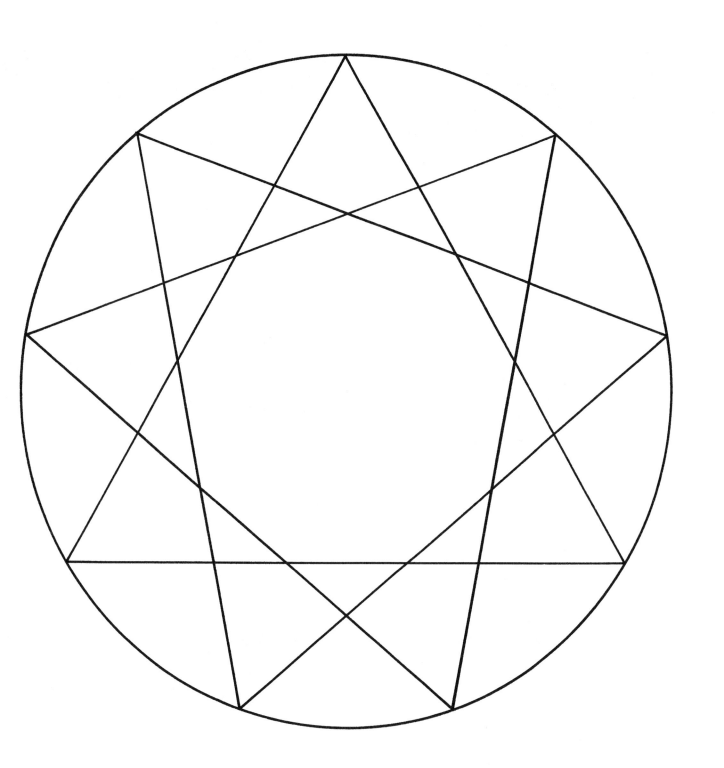

Using lighter colors for the center and shading to darker colors near the outer circle will highlight the radiant potential of this mandala.

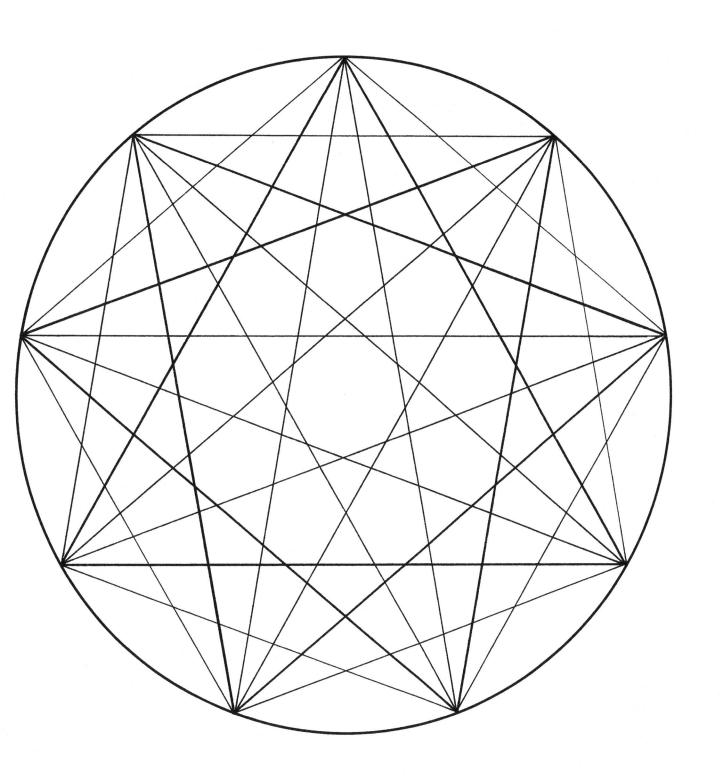

An even-numbered star composed of a single line is unusual.
This design is traditionally associated with stability and protection.

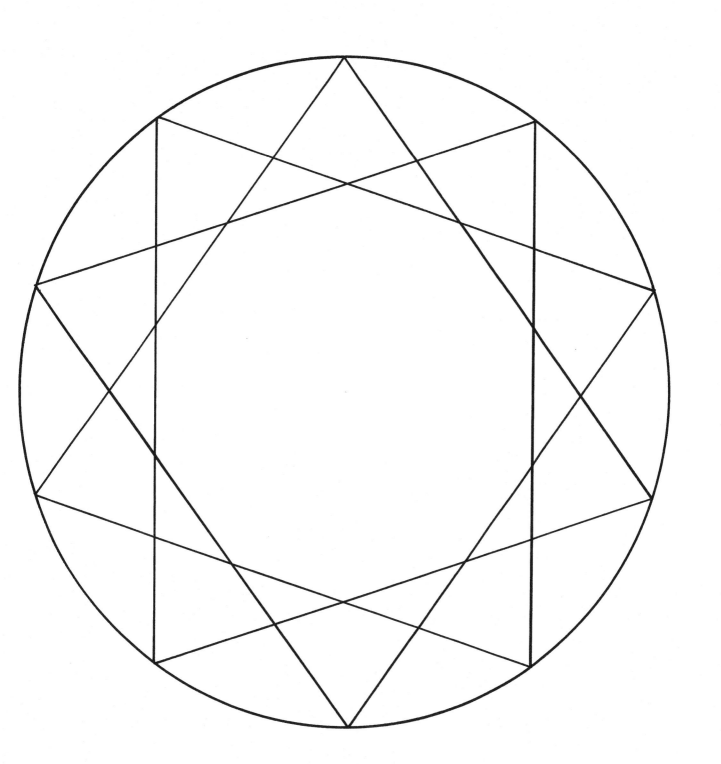

An elegant ten-pointed star, established by a single line, generates visual excitement in this mandala.

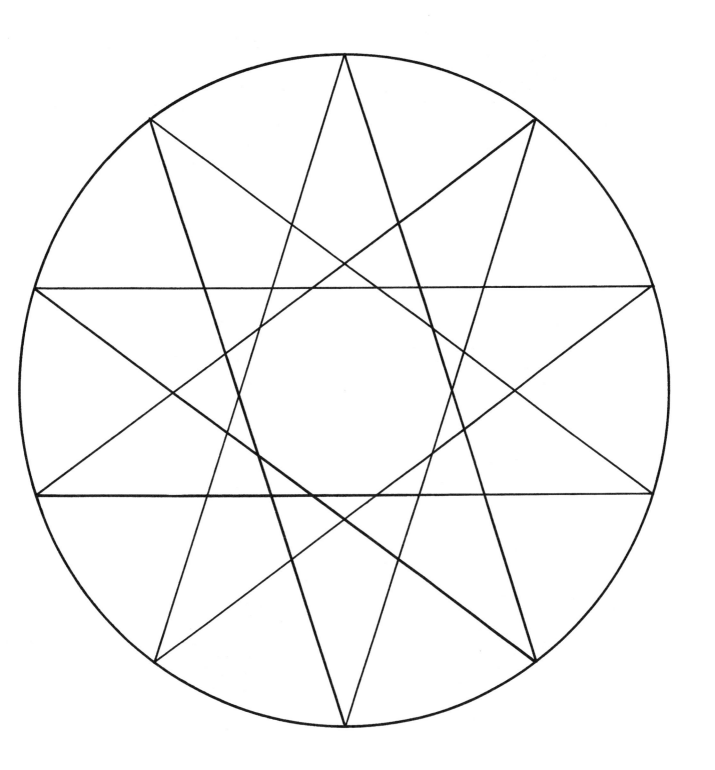

Heightened awareness is induced by visually following the lines in this complex eleven-pointed star.

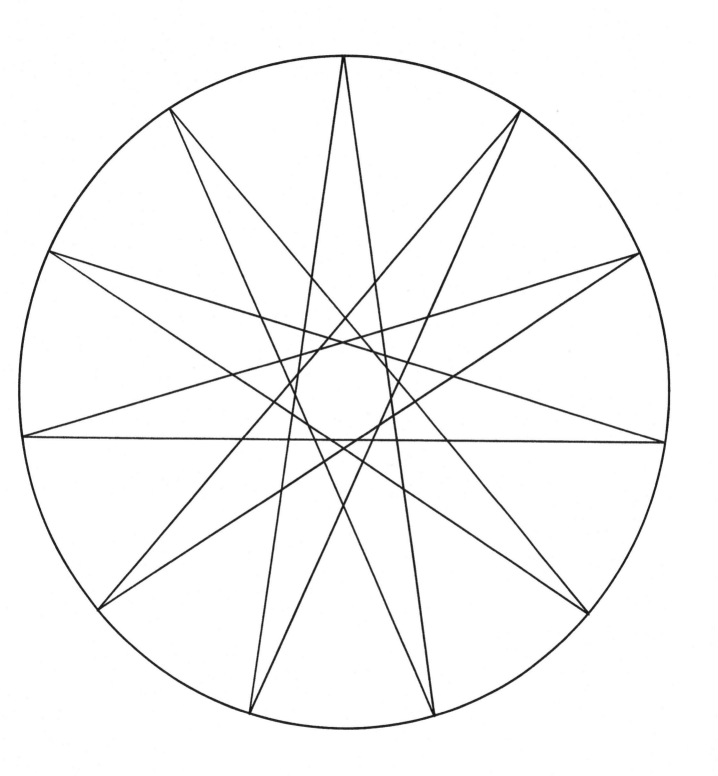

Here we see an example of how a basic mandala star can be elaborated into a more complex mandala. The numbers three, six, and twelve permeate the structure, suggesting activity, beauty, and completion.

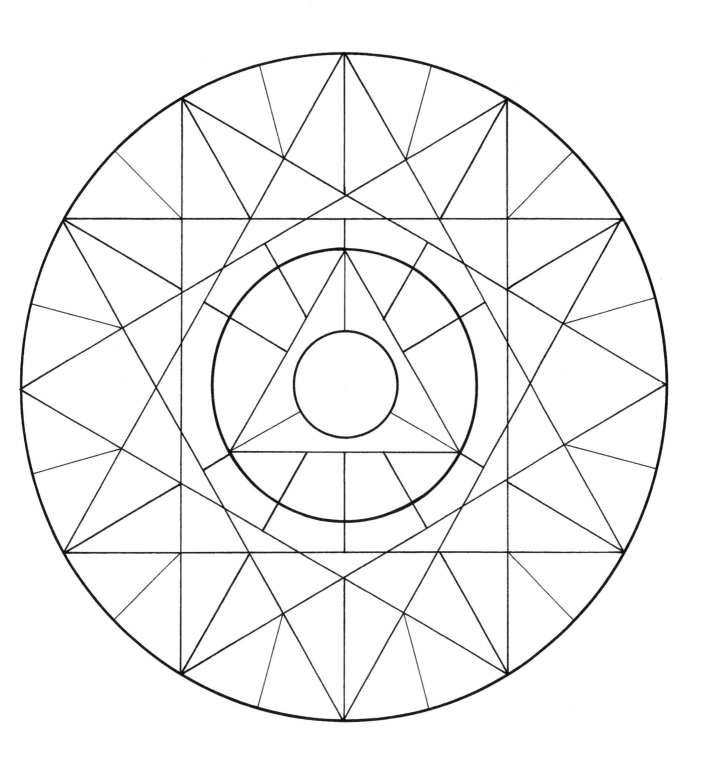

The labyrinth at Chartres Cathedral in France is based on
a thirteen-pointed polygon such as this star mandala. Scribed by
a single line, it poses an invitation to explore possibilities.

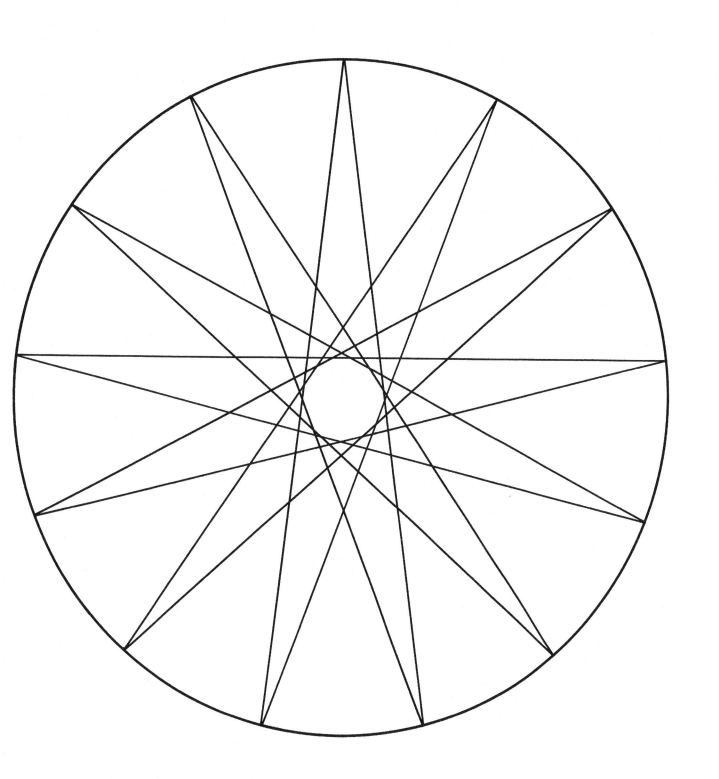

The structure of this mandala is based on the number thirteen, thought by some to be unlucky. However, thirteen is a prime number divisible only by one and itself, making it a numinous entity in sacred geometry. You might enjoy adding lines to connect the two star designs before beginning your coloring process.

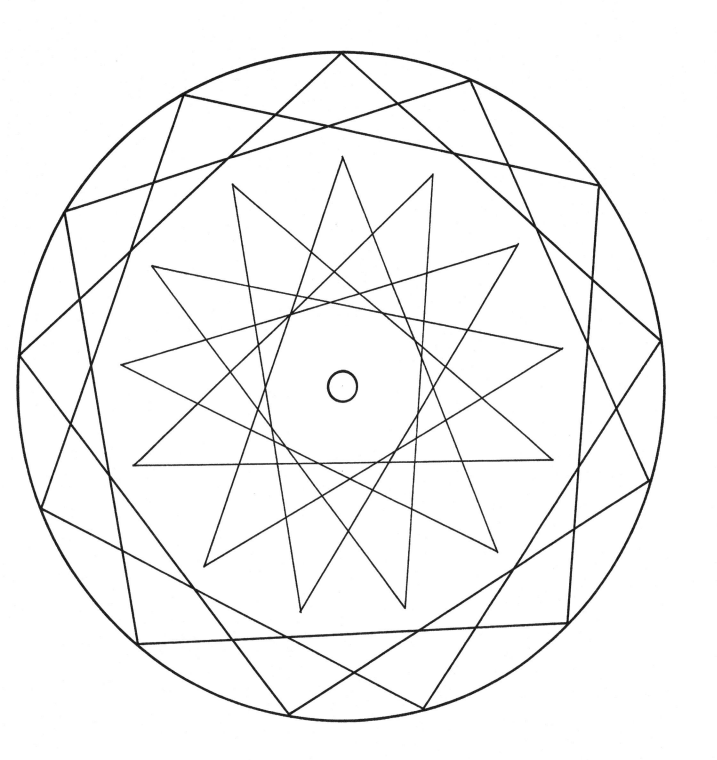

Varied compass settings transformed an ordinary thirteen-pointed star circle into this mandala flurry. Adding colors might just bring on a celebratory mood.

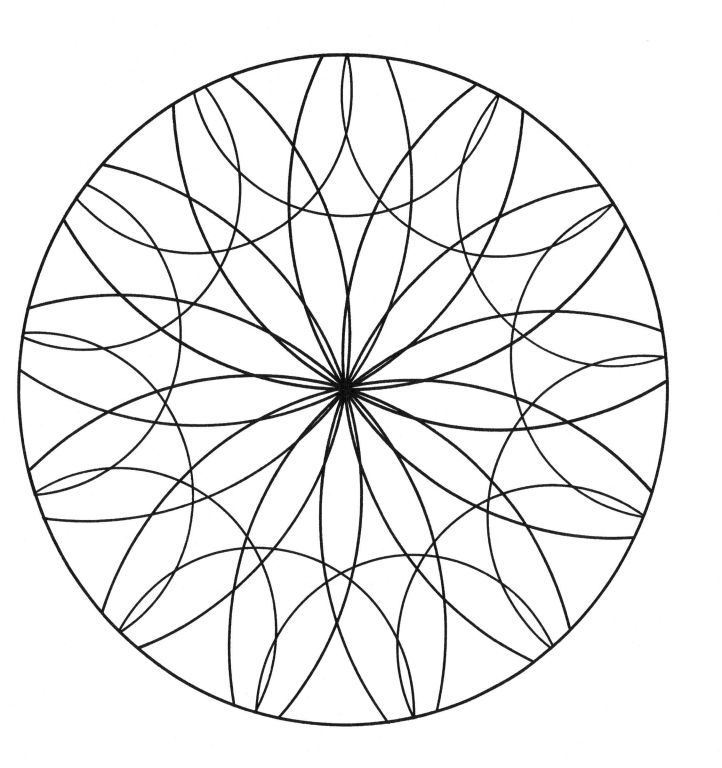

Based on an Islamic pattern, this mandala demonstrates the beautiful complexity of a single ribbon-like line. It illustrates the dictum that *all is one*.

NOTES

A HISTORY OF NUMBERS

1. Seife, Charles, *Zero: The Biography of a Dangerous Idea* (New York: Penguin Putnam, 2000), 71.

2. Ibid., 66.

3. Kaplan, Robert, *The Nothing That Is: A Natural History of Zero* (New York: Oxford University Press, 2000), 100.

4. Nasr, Seyyed Hossein, *Islamic Art and Spirituality* (Albany: State University of New York Press, 1987), 47.

5. Jung, C. G., *Memories, Dreams, Reflections*, ed. Aniela Jaffe, trans. Richard and Clara Winston (New York: Random House, 1965), 196.

6. Cirlot, J. E, *A Dictionary of Symbols* (New York: Philosophical Library, 1962), 193.

7. Tarnas, Richard, *The Passion of the Western Mind* (New York: Ballantine Books, 1991), 425.

8. Hillman, James, *Re-Visioning Psychology* (New York: Harper & Row, 1975), 126.

9. Von Franz, Marie-Louise, *Number and Time* (Evanston, IL: Northwestern University Press, 1986), 45.

THE MEANING BEHIND THE NUMBERS

1. Dudley, Underwood, *Numerology: Or, What Pythagoras Wrought* (Washington, DC: The Mathematical Association of America, 1997), 20.

2. Critchlow, Keith, *Islamic Patterns: An Analytical and Cosmological Approach* (Rochester, VT: Inner Traditions, 1976), 30.

3. Gorman, Peter, *Pythagoras: A Life* (London: Routledge & Kegan Paul, 1979), 144.

4. Schimmel, Annemarie, *The Mystery of Numbers* (New York: Oxford University Press, 1993), 180.

5. Fideler, David R., ed., *The Pythagorean Sourcebook and Library* (Grand Rapids, MI: Phanes Press, 1988), 164.

6. Cirlot, *Dictionary of Symbols,* 335.

7. Ibid., 224.

8. Artress, Lauren, *Walking a Sacred Path: Rediscovering the Labyrinth as a Spiritual Tool* (New York: Riverhead Books, 1995), 64.

DRAWING SACRED GEOMETRY MANDALAS

1. Instructions adapted from Allen, Jon, *Drawing Geometry* (Edinburgh: Floris Books, 2007), 18–19.

2. Walker, Barbara G., *The Woman's Dictionary of Symbols and Sacred Objects* (San Francisco: Harper and Row, 1988), 71.

3. Construction by Daniel Dochery in Dochery, Daniel, "How to Draw a Thirteen-Sided Figure" in Allen, *Drawing Geometry.*

ABOUT THE AUTHOR

SUSANNE F. FINCHER, MA, is a Jungian-oriented psychotherapist, licensed professional counselor, and board-certified art therapist living in Atlanta, Georgia. She is known internationally as an authority on the spiritual, psychological, and health-enhancing dimensions of creativity as expressed in the drawing and coloring of mandalas. Her books on mandalas have been translated into numerous languages. *The Journal of Art Therapy* called *Creating Mandalas* "a classic," and described her Coloring Mandalas series as inviting "a deeper understanding of the cycles of psychological life." More information on Susanne can be found at www.creatingmandalas.com.